Forgiveness: Key to the Kingdom

Forgiveness: Key to the Kingdom

by
Wayne Teafatiller

Treasure House

a division of
Destiny Image
P.O. Box 310
Shippensburg, PA 17257-0310

"For where your treasure is
there will your heart be also." Matthew 6:21

ISBN 1-56043-757-X

For Worldwide Distribution
Printed in the U.S.A.

Destiny Image books are available through these fine distributors outside the United States:

Christian Growth, Inc.
Jalan Kilang-Timor, Singapore 0315

Successful Christian Living
Capetown, Rep. of South Africa

Lifestream
Nottingham, England

Vision Resources
Posonby, Auckland, New Zealand

Rhema Ministries Trading
Randburg, South Africa

WA Buchanan Company
Geebung, Queensland, Australia

Salvation Book Centre
Petaling, Jaya, Malaysia

Word Alive
Niverville, Manitoba, Canada

Dedication

This book is dedicated to the Body of Christ, with special recognition to Pat Shaw and Sandy Dennison for their time given to transcribing it from tapes. I also want to recognize the Body of Christ at New Life Church and thank them for their support and love of the truth.

The Holy Ghost inspired this particular teaching when He stirred up the teaching on forgiveness we received as a part of the Nova Shalom group. The Holy Ghost revealed to me that most of the problems in the world deal with a lack of forgiveness. Whether or not we acknowledge them, those problems still exist and our lives will never have God's peace and joy until we deal with the unforgiveness in our hearts.

Contents

Moreover if thy brother shall trespass against thee, go and tell him his fault between thee and him alone: if he shall hear thee, thou hast gained thy brother. But if he will not hear thee, then take with thee one or two more, that in the mouth of two or three witnesses every word may be established. And if he shall neglect to hear them, tell it unto the church: but if he neglect to hear the church, let him be unto thee as an heathen man and a publican.

Verily I say unto you, Whatsoever ye shall bind on earth shall be bound in heaven: and whatsoever ye shall loose on earth shall be loosed in heaven.

Again I say unto you, That if two of you shall agree on earth as touching any thing that they shall ask, it shall be done for them of my Father which is in heaven. For where two or three are gathered together in my name, there am I in the midst of them.

Then came Peter to him, and said, Lord, how oft shall my brother sin against me, and I forgive him? till seven times?

Jesus saith unto him, I say not unto thee, Until seven times: but, Until seventy times seven.

Therefore is the kingdom of heaven likened unto a certain king, which would take account of his servants. And when he had begun to reckon, one was brought unto him, which owed him ten thousand talents. But forasmuch as he had not to pay, his lord commanded him to be sold, and his wife, and children, and all that he had, and payment to be made.

The servant therefore fell down, and worshipped him, saying, Lord, have patience with me, and I will pay thee all. Then the lord of that servant was moved with compassion, and loosed him, and forgave him the debt.

But the same servant went out, and found one of his fellowservants, which owed him an hundred pence: and he laid hands on him, and took him by the throat, saying, Pay me that thou owest.

And his fellowservant fell down at his feet, and besought him, saying, Have patience with me, and I will pay thee all.

And he would not: but went and cast him into prison, till he should pay the debt. So when his fellowservants saw what was done, they were very sorry, and came and told unto their lord all that was done.

Then his lord, after that he had called him, said unto him, O thou wicked servant, I forgave thee all that debt, because thou desiredst me: Shouldest not thou also have had compassion on thy fellowservant, even as I had pity on thee? And his lord was wroth, and delivered him to the tormentors, till he should pay all that was due unto him.

So likewise shall My heavenly Father do also unto you, if ye from your hearts forgive not every one his brother their trespasses (Matthew 18:15-35).

Introduction

Forgiveness and unforgiveness are, perhaps, the most important themes of our day. Our understanding of the biblical teachings on forgiveness and unforgiveness is directly related to how well or how poorly we are doing in every area of our Christian lives. These mysterious forces can affect our spiritual well-being, our physical health and our financial prosperity. Unforgiveness can wreck marriages and destroy congregations, while forgiveness can restore relationships and bring health and healing to the individual, to the family and to the body of Christ as a whole. What could be more important in the closing days of the twentieth century as we prepare for the end times and the greatest revival the world has ever known?

Webster defines *"to forgive"* as *"to give up resentment against, or the desire to punish; stop being angry with; to pardon; to give all claim to punish or extract penalty for or to cancel or remit."* Such simple words! But they cover a lot of territory, don't they?

I am compelled to put this message into book form because our generation has been tricked by the enemy of our souls into believing that we have the "right" to harbor ill feelings toward others who may have offended us in some way or another. When someone offends us, we are made to believe that we have the "right" to make a "big deal" of that offence. We are convinced that we have the "right" to put the person who has offended us in their place and to demand recourse for the wrongs, real or imagined, that we have suffered. This attitude, so prevalent in our modern society that it is rarely questioned, is completely contrary to the teachings of Jesus. Jesus said: "FORGIVE HIM" (Luke 17:3). And He directly linked our willingness to forgive with His ability to forgive us of our own trespasses.

Indeed, forgiveness is directly linked, in God's Word, to His ability to bless us financially, His ability to answer our prayers, His ability to share with us His power and His gifts and manifestations, and His ability to prosper our home and our marriage.

In teaching us the Lord's Prayer, Jesus made us to know that He forgives us in the same measure that we forgive others. He taught us to pray: "*And forgive us our debts, AS WE FORGIVE OUR DEBTORS*" (Matthew 6:12). What could be more clear?

But could it be correct to say that there is something that God cannot do? He is all-powerful, isn't He? He can do anything, can't He?

As we shall learn in the following pages, we effectively tie the hands of God when we refuse to regard His grace toward us and to extend that grace to others. When we refuse to forgive, we are demonstrating a lack of appreciation for God's forgiveness of our own myriad failures and weaknesses. Our refusal to forgive signals the fact that in our hearts we hold lightly the forgiveness so willingly extended to us through the cross of Christ. There can be no greater offense before God. No wonder this sin can rob us of all our blessings!

Several years ago I began to preach systematically to my congregation about forgiveness. The most important reason I preached it to them was that God had been dealing with my own life about forgiveness. I began studying all that the Bible has to say on the subject. And the more I learned about forgiveness, the more I wanted to learn. The more I studied, the more God spoke to my own heart. As forgiveness began to work effectively in my own life, I began sharing it with my own congregation. As I did, I discovered that I was onto something BIG, bigger than anything I had ever studied or taught before.

About that time I was experiencing some problems with one of my feet. It often left me in great pain, and it was difficult for me to put on my shoes. When I would minister in the church about forgiveness, however, the pain would disappear. I hadn't realized that I had areas of unforgiveness in my own life.

Many of the things God taught me in those days I seemed to be hearing for the first time, almost as if I had never read the Bible. I got very excited about what I was learning and very excited in sharing it with others. As I taught from week to week in my church, developing the theme as I went, and learning much more myself as I taught it to others, many of my members came to me and told me that their lives had been changed by what they were learning. I knew what they meant. This message has also changed my life.

When I say, therefore, that this is a powerful message, I know what I am talking about. I have experienced its power in my own life and in the life of my members. I present it now to the Body of Christ with the prayer that it may be a vehicle of sincere change that will bring us from bitterness into rejoicing, from sickness to health and from need to true prosperity. This is your day to forgive and to be forgiven.

Pastor Wayne Teafatiller
Woodsfield, Ohio

Part I

The Little Understood Concept of Christian Forgiveness

Chapter 1

Forgiveness and Unforgiveness: Powerful Seeds That Produce a Harvest

And He began again to teach by the sea side: and there was gathered unto Him a great multitude, so that He entered into a ship, and sat in the sea; and the whole multitude was by the sea on the land. And He taught them many things by parables, and said unto them in His doctrine, Hearken; Behold, there went out a sower to sow. (Mark 4:1-3)

When Jesus began His teachings of the well-known Parable of the Sower, "*a great multitude*" was listening. As He continued, however, the crowd dwindled, until only the disciples remained. Even they were not sure of the full meaning of Jesus' teachings and asked Him to explain. He explained to them why not everyone understood what He said.

*And when He was alone, they that were about
Him with the twelve asked of Him the parable.
And He said unto them, Unto you it is given to
know the mystery of the kingdom of God: but
unto them that are without, all these things are
done in parables.* (Mark 4:10-11)

What Jesus told these disciples may come as a
surprise to many. God's mysteries are not for everyone. They are hidden to the many and revealed to the
few who have a heart toward Him. His use of parables
had a two-fold purpose. The parable was a simple way
of conveying God's truths to the sincere and an equally
simple way of hiding those same truths from those
who only pretended to be interested.

*That seeing they may see, and not perceive; and
hearing they may hear, and not understand; lest
at any time they should be converted, and their
sins should be forgiven them.* (Mark 4:12)

Access to the Kingdom of God is not for everyone.
But the most amazing statement that Jesus made is
recorded in the very next verse:

*And He said unto them, Know ye not this par-
able? and how then will ye know all parables*?
(Mark 4:13)

There is something about this parable that explains all parables. There is a truth here that unlocks
all truths. There is some knowledge to be had here
that makes all other knowledge accessible to the
believer. That great and all-important secret is the law

of sowing and reaping. It is explained in God's Word as follows:

Be not deceived; God is not mocked: for what-soever a man soweth, that shall he also reap. (Galatians 6:7)

But this I say, He which soweth sparingly shall reap also sparingly; and he which soweth boun-tifully shall reap also bountifully. (II Corin-thians 9:6)

Seeds are powerful. Seeds are important. When planted— intentionally or unintentionally—they pro-duce a harvest. Seeds have a life of their own. Once they are planted, an automatic, God-designed process is put into motion. And the result of that process is a harvest. Good seeds produce, and bad seeds produce. And seeds can grow amazingly overnight. By morning, sometimes we have forgotten that the seed was ever sown. But the seed is not hindered by our lack of remembrance. It has already germinated. And it goes on in the process of growing and developing. The longer you forget that seed the more amazed you will be when one day you see the plant it has produced.

The life that comes forth from a seed can grow at an alarming rate. We usually don't use that term "alarm-ing" because when we talk about seeds, we are talking about good seeds and good results, so it isn't alarming at all. The production of good seeds is wonderful. Farmers have often been very religious people because they can't help but see the hand of God in the seeds they plant and the harvests they reap as a result. But, alas, not all seeds are good. There are both good and bad seeds. There are seeds of the Spirit and seeds of the flesh.

> *This I say then, Walk in the Spirit, and ye shall not fulfil the lust of the flesh. For the flesh lusteth against the Spirit, and the Spirit against the flesh: and these are contrary the one to the other: so that ye cannot do the things that ye would. But if ye be led of the Spirit, ye are not under the law. Now the works of the flesh are manifest, which are these; Adultery, fornication, uncleanness, lasciviousness, Idolatry, witchcraft, hatred, variance, emulations, wrath, strife, seditions, heresies, Envyings, murders, drunkenness, revellings, and such like: of the which I tell you before, as I have also told you in time past, that they which do such things shall not inherit the kingdom of God.* (Galatians 5:16-21)

If you can't find your particular bad seed in the first list, you will find it in the words *"such like."* These are powerful and dangerous seeds that, if given opportunity, will produce a terrible harvest. Thank God that we can sow good seed through a life in the Spirit.

> *But the fruit of the Spirit is love, joy, peace, longsuffering, gentleness, goodness, faith.* (Galatians 5:22)

These are also powerful seeds, but the harvest they produce is very different.

> *For he that soweth to his flesh shall of the flesh reap corruption; but he that soweth to the Spirit shall of the Spirit reap life everlasting. And let*

*us not be weary in well doing: for in due season
we shall reap, if we faint not.* (Galatians 6:8-9)

The law of sowing and reaping is one of the most
prominent in the Bible. It never fails. What is sown
will eventually produce—for good or for bad.

What does all of this have to do with forgiveness
and unforgiveness? Forgiveness is a seed, a powerful
seed that produces a wonderful crop. And unforgiveness is also a seed, an equally powerful seed, an evil
seed that produces a terrible harvest. The writer to
the Hebrews warned the believers of the early church
to beware of seeds that might produce in them a *"root
of bitterness."* Such a root, he warned, had been the
reason that many had been *"defiled."*

*Looking diligently lest any man fail of the grace
of God; lest any root of bitterness springing up
trouble you, and thereby many be defiled.*
(Hebrews 12:15)

Roots have a way of taking over everything around
them. They are so strong that they can destroy foundations and wreck buildings. Once roots are allowed to
grow, they are extremely difficult to get rid of. They
thrust deep down below the surface and gain a powerful hold that is not easily relinquished.

What are the subtle seeds that can grow into
powerful roots that can destroy our souls? Amazingly,
we call them by fairly innocuous names. We call them
"hurts" or "hurt feelings." We call them "disappointments." We call them "wounds" or "wounded spirits."
The Bible calls them *"offenses"* or *"trespasses"* or

"debts." Whatever we call them, the meaning is clear. Someone has wronged us.

The problem with such "offenses," these days, is that we are encouraged by the spirit of our times to think that we have a right to make a big thing out of them and to demand that the wrong be righted. This attitude has resulted in our becoming the most litigious society in history, suing each other for every slight—real or imagined.

We whip simple slights, simple hurts, simple disappointments into jealousy, anger and resentment. We let simple seeds grow into serious plants that can do ourselves and those around us much harm.

But this attitude, so prevalent in our modern society, is far from the basis of Christian concept laid down by Christ Himself. He said:

> *...forgive, if ye have ought against any....* (Mark 11:25)

"Ought" means *"anything."* The Christian way is not to demand our right to harbor ill will against those who have wronged us and to build upon that wrong. The Christian way is to forgive. As Christians, we are even commanded to show kindness to our enemies.

> *But I say unto you, Love your enemies, bless them that curse you, do good to them that hate you, and pray for them which despitefully use you, and persecute you.* (Matthew 5:44)

If we are to show kindness to our enemies, how much more important it is to show kindness to the people we love, those we come in contact with daily!

Yet, those are the very people who often offend us. It is not uncommon to see deep-seated hurts develop between husband and wife, parents and their children, brothers and sisters, between in-laws, between employers and their employees, between neighbors, and even between pastors and their members. The people we love have the potential for hurting us more than anyone else. And these hurts, if left unattended, are the deadly seeds that sprout and grow and produce root systems which choke the life out of us.

As we are going to see, such simple seeds affect everything about our lives. They affect the welfare of our souls and our continued relationship to God, our physical and mental health, our financial prosperity, our marriage, our home, our other relationships and our comfort or lack of it within the larger Body of Christ. This is serious business that demands our immediate attention.

If a seed has been planted and is allowed to grow, expect to reap the crop. It makes no difference that you forget what is planted. Farmers often have to mark rows to remind themselves what is planted there. They can easily forget. But it doesn't matter. If you forget a seed, it just keeps on growing. Nothing stops it. If you want to stop it, you have to purposefully pull it up by the roots. And if you don't do that, expect to reap the results.

In other areas, we have learned this lesson:

My little children, these things write I unto you, that ye sin not. And if any man sin, we have an advocate with the Father, Jesus Christ the righteous. (I John 2:1)

Many of us have learned about the dangers of sin in our everyday Christian lives. We have learned that when we have committed any sin, we must confess that sin to the Father. He is not only ready to forgive us but is ready to act as our Advocate. By confessing our sins and asking God to forgive us we rob satan of the opportunity to put his foot into the door of our souls. What a powerful lesson!

Now, we must learn the equally powerful lesson that when we refuse to forgive those who have offended us in some way, we are showing disdain for the grace of God that has forgiven us of our own offenses. If God has forgiven us so much, how can we fail to forgive another something much less significant? Thus, unforgiveness becomes a serious offense in the eyes of God. It is a slap in His face, and He cannot overlook it.

Unforgiveness is the worst of sins. When a person commits adultery or fornication, they sin against their own body. But, when you fail to appreciate God's mercy and to extend it to others, you grieve the heart of God and cut off His hand of favor on your behalf. Unforgiveness not only separates you from God. It robs you of the promises of God for your life...in every way.

You can quote verses from the Bible all you want, but if your heart is filled with unforgiveness, God cannot bless you. You can do good works all you want, but if your heart is filled with unforgiveness, God cannot bless you.

Contrary to popular belief, you have no right to hold unforgiveness in your heart. It doesn't matter what anyone has done to you or said to you, you have no right to maintain a grudge against them. God has extended to you His forgiveness. Now He expects you to extend it to others...no matter what may be the circumstances. If you refuse and continue to harbor a seed of bitterness or resentment in your heart, you are only asking for trouble.

A little bit of bitterness doesn't seem like such a dangerous thing. A little bit of anger doesn't seem like such a dangerous thing. That may be true. A little seed of corn doesn't seem like anything significant. But one tiny seed corn can produce hundreds of identical kernels.

Some people are afraid to face these things. They would rather ignore them and hope they go away. But, if something is hindering me from walking in the best that God has for me, I want to know about it. I want it dug up. I want it exposed. I want to get rid of that thing. I don't want to give the devil something to use against me.

Some people are suffering because of something that happened to them many years ago. They are being robbed because of something another person did or said. That doesn't make sense, doesn't it? Why should I suffer for the wrongs of others? This is satan's trick to destroy us.

Personally, I am determined not to let anything separate me from the love of God. It's not worth it. I refuse to lose out because of the errors of others. I refuse to suffer for something someone else did to me, however bad it might have been.

But am I always aware that a seed has been planted and is even now growing? I discovered that sometimes I am not. Many of us don't understand the things that are happening to us. We forget that some seeds were planted. We forget that seeds always produce. We forget that we reap what we sow. We forget that we failed to deal with a certain situation and we let that seed go on growing, until it is often too late. When least expected that plant explodes to the surface in rages that destroy our marriages, wreck our professional careers and send us into the depths of depression. What is the answer?

The answer is to nip that thing in the bud before it has a chance to flower and bring forth fruit. Otherwise, you will pay the consequences. The answer is to recognize unforgiveness for the dangerous seed it is. The answer is to recognize how offensive it is to God when we refuse to forgive the minor offenses of another when He has forgiven our major offenses.

Some people want God, in a moment's time, to get them out of messes they have been creating for themselves for years. And many times He refuses. He allows us to go through a process of undoing, a process that signals to God that we now understand the law of sowing and reaping and that we are ready to plant a proper crop in the future and to prevent the sprouting of damaging seeds in our souls.

Asking forgiveness from God for your own offenses jerks the offending plant out by the roots and gives it no chance to produce further havoc. Forgiving others of their offenses toward us does exactly the same thing. Failing to forgive brings disastrous results.

Unforgiveness usually starts out as something very small. But it has a way of growing and multiplying. Before long, it is something very large. It is a deadly poison, a fatal cancer, a dangerous disease.

But don't we have the "right" to be hurt, to feel offended, to nurse a wounded spirit and to expect redress of all wrongs? Legally, we may have the right. But, spiritually, we can't afford it. The cost is too high.

According to the system of the world we have every right to maintain our hard feelings. We are encouraged to do so. According to the ever broadening definition of human rights, personal rights and religious rights, we have every "right" to feel the way we do; but we simply cannot afford to pursue the wrong. Believe me. We can never win by pursuing the wrongs done to us. We can only lose.

Jesus said, "FORGIVE." As we have seen, that means *"to give up resentment, or the desire to punish, to stop being angry with, to pardon, to give up all claim to punish or extract penalty for an offense, to cancel or remit the debt."* No, you have no right to maintain bitterness in your heart. No, you have no right to harbor ill will toward another. By accepting the unconditional forgiveness of Christ for your own life, you have forfeited the right to hold anything against anyone else...no matter what they have done to you or said about you.

Whether the offending person has repented before God or not is not our business. That is between them and God. Our business is to make sure that whatever offense has been committed against us personally has not left some bad influence upon our own souls.

The future of the offender depends on his or her own reaction. Nothing we can do will change that. Either people repent and receive forgiveness from God or they resist and suffer the consequence. But, whatever their decision, ours must always be the same. Their decision must not affect our own.

If the offender is repentant or not is inconsequential. I will forgive...whether the desired response is present in the other person or not. So, whatever other people do or do not do will not affect me personally. I am the arbiter of my own destiny. My future is between me and God. No one else can hinder me.

Because of this, my destiny does not depend on whether I was born into a good family or a bad family. I decide my own destiny by taking advantage of the good in my life and by rejecting the bad that comes my way. It is my decision.

If people are sorry for offending us and ask our forgiveness, so much the better...for them. But if they don't, we lose nothing. Either way we win. Recognizing the danger of allowing the seed of unforgiveness to fall into the ground and sprout, Paul taught the church at Ephesus:

> ...*let not the sun go down upon your wrath.* (Ephesians 4:26)

Not even one day must be allowed to pass with that bad seed in the ground. It is too dangerous. By harboring unforgiveness, you are opening yourself up to the devil. And, when you open yourself up to the devil, he can manifest many evil things in your life. You must live free from his power. You must not give him any place in your life. Paul continued:

Neither give place to the devil. (Ephesians 4:27)

If an evil seed is allowed to remain in the earth, something that is said or done may water it and give it life. If you had dug it up immediately, there would be nothing to water, but the fact that it has been allowed to grow gives it something to build on. You can't afford to take that chance. Satan is too astute. He will take advantage of any opening you give him. Jerk up that seed. Give it no place. Forgive.

Chapter 2

Forgiveness and Unforgiveness: Binding and Loosing

Then was brought unto Him one possessed with a devil, blind, and dumb: and He healed him, insomuch that the blind and dumb both spake and saw. And all the people were amazed, and said, Is not this the son of David? But when the Pharisees heard it, they said, This fellow doth not cast out devils, but by Beelzebub the prince of the devils. And Jesus knew their thoughts, and said unto them, Every kingdom divided against itself is brought to desolation; and every city or house divided against itself shall not stand: And if Satan cast out Satan, he is divided against himself; how shall then his kingdom stand? And if I by Beelzebub cast out devils, by whom do your children cast them out? therefore they shall be your judges. But if I cast out devils by the Spirit of God, then the kingdom of God is come unto you. Or else how can one enter into a strong

*man's house, and spoil his goods, except he first
bind the strong man? and then he will spoil his
house. He that is not with Me is against Me; and
he that gathereth not with Me scattereth abroad.*
(Matthew 12:22-30)

The popular concept of binding and loosing is that
we, in God's authority, take power over the devil and
bind him. Having done this, we loose upon ourselves
and others God's blessings. I find little biblical proof
for this popular teaching.

Jesus rebuked the devil and told him, *"Get thee behind me"* (Matthew 16:23 & Luke 4:8). We can do the
same. James wrote to the church:

*Submit yourselves therefore to God. Resist the
devil, and he will flee from you.* (James 4:7)

Jesus cast out demon spirits and brought deliver-
ance to those who were bound by them.

*When the even was come, they brought unto Him
many that were possessed with devils: and He
cast out the spirits with His word, and healed all
that were sick.* (Matthew 8:16)

He taught us to cast out demons too:

*Heal the sick, cleanse the lepers, raise the dead,
cast out devils: freely ye have received, freely
give.* (Matthew 10:8)

In fact, casting out devils (demons) is the first mentioned of the *"signs"* which Jesus said should follow
all believers.

And these signs shall follow them that believe; In My name shall they cast out devils.... (Mark 16:17)

But rebuking the devil and casting out demons is very different from binding satan. Can satan be bound? One day he will be bound and cast into the Lake of Fire (Revelation 19:20), but until then we cannot bind him. He has a God-ordained work to perform. He is to test every believer and to provide an alternative for those who reject God.

Try to find one place in the Bible where Jesus bound satan. You won't find it. It doesn't exist. Until all things are placed under the feet of Jesus, satan has certain rights here on this earth. He has been dealt with spiritually, but he has not yet been dealt with physically. And he cannot be bound until his time. Therefore, all the time we spend binding the devil is in vain. We must spend that time on something fruitful, something possible.

So, what did Jesus mean by "bind," and what are we supposed to be binding? He said:

Moreover if thy brother shall trespass against thee, go and tell him his fault between thee and him alone: if he shall hear thee, thou hast gained thy brother. But if he will not hear thee, then take with thee one or two more, that in the mouth of two or three witnesses every word may be established. And if he shall neglect to hear them, tell it unto the church: but if he neglect to hear the church, let him be unto thee as an heathen man and a publican. Verily I say unto you, Whatsoever

*ye shall bind on earth shall be bound in heaven:
and whatsoever ye shall loose on earth shall be
loosed in heaven.* (Matthew 18:15-18)

Did I miss something here? Did he say something
about the devil? I don't see it. This truth is not about the
devil. This is about you and me. This is about forgiving
one another. This is about not harboring ill feelings
toward one another. We need to worry less about the
devil and worry more about our own spiritual condition.

When we resist the devil, he has no power over us.
Satan is not the strong man with whom we need to
concern ourselves. You are your own worst enemy. You
are master of your own destiny. You are robbing yourself of the blessings of God. Get yourself under control,
and satan will have no place in your life.

If I am free, no one can bind me. I am the only one
who can bind up my own life by the unforgiveness I
harbor in my heart. If I do it, I willingly hand over the
key to my house and all that is mine to the enemy of my
soul. Nine out of ten times the devil isn't our problem.
We are the problem. Unforgiveness is our problem.

Satan is not your problem. You are the problem. You
need to forgive your husband. You need to forgive your
wife. You need to forgive your children. You need to forgive your father. You need to forgive your mother. You
need to forgive your boss. You need to forgive everyone
that has offended you in any way whatsoever.

Jesus went on to show the power produced by forgiveness and the resultant harmony among brothers:

*Again I say unto you, That if two of you shall
agree on earth as touching any thing that they
shall ask, it shall be done for them of My Father*

which is in heaven. For where two or three are gathered together in My name, there am I in the midst of them. (Matthew 18:19-20)

Binding and loosing is directly related to forgiveness and unforgiveness. When I fail to forgive someone the offenses committed against me, I bind the hands of God on my behalf. This slight of His grace cannot go unnoticed. He cannot bless me until I repent of my lack of forgiveness. In this way, I effectively bind the hands of God. Forgiveness brings loosing.

In Thayers [#3089 Matt. 16:19; To declare lawful; Matt. 18:18], I found the following definition: *"To loose is to declare lawful."* If something is lawful, God can move on it. He can act. His power is loosed. God doesn't move outside of the legal. He acts when we get in line with His Word. He has declared His express will for unity among brothers. When we get in unity with our brothers and sisters, all the power of hell cannot stop the blessing of God from coming upon our lives. We loose the hands of God in our own behalf.

The promise is that whatever you ask *"IT SHALL BE DONE,"* but there is a condition. It will happen when you get into agreement with your brother, when you cease to tie the hands of God on your behalf. And it is unforgiveness that ties God's hands.

To loose means *"to permit or allow."* Let God bless you like He wants to. Let Him have His way in your life. Even animosity against an enemy can hinder your spiritual blessing. In the Sermon on the Mount, Jesus had said:

Agree with thine adversary quickly, whiles thou art in the way with him; lest at any time

*the adversary deliver thee to the judge, and the
judge deliver thee to the officer, and thou be cast
into prison.* (Matthew 5:25)

How powerful! Don't even keep anything in your
heart against your enemies. You bind by unforgiveness, and you loose by forgiveness.

We have always assumed that this *"strong man"*
was the devil. But Jesus never called satan strong. He
said: *"All power is given unto Me in heaven and in
earth"* (Matthew 28:18). The only power satan has is
the power God gives him, and that is given only for a
specific purpose and for a specific time.

I am the strong man over my household. I am the
one who determines whether my house will be blessed
or cursed. If the devil wants to steal my goods, he first
has to bind me. Only I have the power to bind or loose
the hands of God on my own behalf.

It is terrible when a person you love, perhaps a
child, ties your hands through their disobedience or
rebellion and prevents you from helping them! How
must God feel when we tie His hands of blessing?

When you say, "I forgive," that unties the hands of
God, and He can respond, "You are forgiven." He can
also say, "Rise up and walk! Be healed! Receive your
sight!" and many other wonderful things, as well...as
we will explore in Part II.

Nothing is impossible for God and He can bless you
no matter what. But He has chosen not to respond
when you despise His grace. When you fail to forgive,
therefore, you effectively tie the hands of God. If you

are not willing to forgive your brother some minor offense when God, in His great mercy, has forgiven you so much, then He will not and cannot bless you.

You need not live under the thumb of satan. He was not destined to rule over you. You were destined to be God's child and to share in His glory. But you must decide. If you want to prevent the devil from having power over your life, start forgiving as Christ has forgiven you. That will rob satan of his intent upon your life.

Paul's concern, in writing to the Ephesians, was:

That we henceforth be no more children, tossed to and fro, and carried about with every wind of doctrine, by the sleight of men, and cunning craftiness, whereby they lie in wait to deceive; But speaking the truth in love, may grow up into him in all things, which is the head, even Christ. (Ephesians 4:14- 15)

We need to *"grow up into Him in all things."* That requires maturity in thought and action. That requires laying aside pettiness and unforgiveness and acting like adults for a change.

Forgiveness is a powerful force. Jesus said:

Whosoever sins ye remit, they are remitted unto them; and whosoever sins ye retain, they are retained. (John 20:23)

To *"remit"* means *"to forgive, to pardon, to cancel,* or *to release."* To *"retain"* is *"to keep in a fixed state or condition, to hold or keep in possession."* God has placed great power in our hands.

Does that mean that we have the power to forgive sins? Certainly not! Only God can forgive sins. What, then, are we remitting? And what, then, are we retaining? Since God is the only one who can forgive a person's sins, this passage necessarily means that we have the power to forgive or not forgive the offenses committed against us personally. We can choose not to forgive. In that case, we "retain" their sin, we keep their offense in a fixed state or condition and hold or keep it in possession. This is the fastest way known to man to cut off God's blessing upon your own life.

We can choose to forgive. When we do, we are pardoning, canceling or releasing our rights to redress; and, at the same time, we are loosing the hands of God on our behalf. This is the quickest way known to man to be blessed.

The secret, then, of binding and loosing is the ability to forgive. What does it mean to *"bind?"* It means *"to prohibit, to prevent or to hinder."* When we fail to forgive others, we are preventing or hindering God from moving on our behalf.

What we "bind" on earth in unforgiveness keeps God's blessings "bound" in heaven and what we "loose" on earth in forgiveness allows God to let loose His blessings to flow down from Him to us.

What are you waiting for? Forgive and be blessed.

Chapter 3

Forgiveness and Unforgiveness: Keys to the Kingdom of Heaven

And I will give unto thee the keys of the kingdom of heaven: and whatsoever thou shalt bind on earth shall be bound in heaven: and whatsoever thou shalt loose on earth shall be loosed in heaven. (Matthew 16:19)

The power to bind and loose, the power to forgive or not forgive represents, Jesus said, *"the keys of the kingdom of heaven."* As believers, we are always looking for keys that will unlock the mysteries of God's Word to us. We have long dwelt on prayer and fasting as one of those important keys. The gifts of the Spirit unlock many mysteries to us. The marvel of preaching unlocks many mysteries to us. And revelation, in the form of dreams and visions and other types of supernatural insight, also unlocks God's treasure chest to us. Here we discover two more of those important keys...forgiveness and unforgiveness.

Some keys don't look very impressive. They are not terribly valuable in themselves. They are not often things of beauty. But, when we consider what lies behind the doors that keys can unlock, we know that they are much more valuable than they might seem. Just lose your car key or your house key or your locker key or your pass key and you will soon realize how valuable that little piece of metal can be. Like many other things in life, we sometimes have to lose a key to appreciate its value.

Yes, in itself, the key seems to be fairly common and void of great significance. But, given its power to unlock and open to us vast treasures, we soon discover that nothing is more important than a key. And forgiveness is one of the most important of keys. Bind it about your neck. Keep it close. And don't lose it, whatever you do.

I don't know about you, but I am determined to walk in victory in my Christian life. I am determined to utilize the keys God has placed in my hands.

What sort of doors will this key open? It will open doors to peace and joy, doors to health and happiness, doors to prosperity and riches...and much more. This is the key to the anointing of God. This is the key to His power. This is the key to unity in the church. This is the key to maturity. Learn to use this key well.

And to the angel of the church in Philadelphia write; These things saith He that is holy, He that is true, He that hath the key of David, He that openeth, and no man shutteth; and shutteth, and no man openeth; I know thy works: behold, I

*have set before thee an open door, and no man
can shut it: for thou hast a little strength, and
hast kept my word, and hast not denied my
name. Behold, I will make them of the synagogue
of Satan, which say they are Jews, and are not,
but do lie; behold, I will make them to come and
worship before thy feet, and to know that I have
loved thee. Because thou hast kept the word of
My patience, I also will keep thee from the hour
of temptation, which shall come upon all the
world, to try them that dwell upon the earth.*
(Revelation 3:7-10)

Each of the seven churches of Revelation represent
a phase of the Church on earth. In every age God has
been preparing His people to be united with Him for
eternity. Of each of the seven churches God had something bad to say, except of the church of Philadelphia.
The Church at Philadelphia, the Church of Brotherly
Love, had a key which was called *"the key of David."*
This key was said to be powerful. When it opened a
door, no man could shut that door; and when it shut a
door, no man could open that door. As we will learn in
Part III, David's secret was a forgiving heart. He, in
fact, was called *"a man after His* [God's] *own heart"*
(I Samuel 13:4). Therefore, *"the key of David"* is the
key of forgiveness.

You have the key to the kingdom of heaven. You
can open doors and you can close doors. Forgiveness
opens doors, and unforgiveness closes doors. It is that
simple.

This key works. It *"openeth."* When you forgive, you
are opening the door to God's blessings, and no one has

the power to close that door. But when you shut that door by your refusal to reciprocate God's mercy, no one else can open that door, not even Jesus. You have the key. He has given it to you.

The Church of Philadelphia only had a little strength. Nevertheless, this church prevailed because it relied on the strength of God Almighty. The members of the Church of Philadelphia had kept the Word of the Lord. They had refused to harbor ill will in their hearts against their neighbor. They had refused to give place to the enemy by allowing seeds of discord to grow up in their spirits. In so doing, they had refused to deny the Lord's name.

Because of that, the Lord promised to keep them in difficult times. No time in history could be more correctly labeled "the hour of temptation" than the day in which you and I are now entering. We can't afford to play church any longer, friends. The time of the end is upon us. We need to press into God's favor in order to stand in the difficult times that are coming upon us.

The Lord warned this church:

Behold, I come quickly: hold that fast which thou hast, that no man take thy crown. Him that overcometh will I make a pillar in the temple of My God, and he shall go no more out: and I will write upon him the name of My God, and the name of the city of My God, which is new Jerusalem, which cometh down out of heaven from My God: and I will write upon him My new name. (Revelation 3:11-12)

John was privileged to see the final outcome. He was privileged to see that the Bride of Christ did prepare herself and was joined with the Bridegroom, becoming a pillar, a permanent fixture, in the temple of God. Thank God for that revelation. It will be accomplished only through using the keys God has entrusted into our hands.

Isaiah prophesied of this same key:

And I will clothe Him with thy robe, and strengthen Him with thy girdle, and I will commit thy government into His hand: and He shall be a father to the inhabitants of Jerusalem, and to the house of Judah. And the key of the house of David will I lay upon His shoulder; so He shall open, and none shall shut; and He shall shut, and none shall open. (Isaiah 22:21-22)

He called this key *"the key of the house of David."* What would this key do? It would *"open"* and when it had opened something, no one could shut it. This key also could shut, and when it had shut, *"none shall open."*

I am convinced of which the prophets prophesied and which John saw in his revelation on the Isle of Patmos was none other than forgiveness. This key has the power to lock doors so well that none can open them and to unlock doors so that none has the power to shut them. And God has placed it in your hands.

No devil has enough power to deter us when we walk in forgiveness. And no one has the power to bless us when we refuse to do so. You hold the keys. What are you waiting for? Forgive.

.

Chapter 4

Forgiveness: The Greatest Love Story Ever Told

Repent ye: for the kingdom of heaven is at hand. (Matthew 3:2)

When John the Baptist appeared and began to preach his message of repentance, people didn't think that his message was very loving. But Jesus (who was God in the flesh, and *"God is love"*... I John 4:6) essentially preached the same message.

Repent ye, and believe the gospel. (Mark 1:15)

Repentance is a loving message. If we love someone, we want the best for them. We want them to be blessed. We want them to prosper under the mighty hand of God. And, in order for them to prosper, we know that they must first be forgiven and that they must be forgiving. Forgiveness is the greatest love story ever told.

Jesus came to forgive. He lived a life of forgiveness, as an example to us. The Pharisees wanted to stone a woman who had been taken in the act of adultery, but

Jesus reminded them of their own sins and said, *"He that is without sin among you, let him first cast a stone at her"* (John 8:7). When each of her accusers crept silently away, unwilling to face his own failings, Jesus turned to the woman and said:

> *Neither do I condemn thee: go, and sin no more.* (John 8:11)

Jesus did not come to earth to condemn. He came to redeem. That redemption took the form of forgiveness. To the impotent man who had been healed at the Pool of Bethesda, His message was the same:

> *Behold, thou art made whole: sin no more, lest a worse thing come unto thee.* (John 5:14)

Jesus was Himself forgiving, and He taught His disciples to be forgiving too. He told them to be like a little child, quickly forgetting offenses.

> *At the same time came the disciples unto Jesus, saying, Who is the greatest in the kingdom of heaven? And Jesus called a little child unto Him, and set him in the midst of them, And said, Verily I say unto you, Except ye be converted, and become as little children, ye shall not enter into the kingdom of heaven. Whosoever therefore shall humble himself as this little child, the same is greatest in the kingdom of heaven. And whoso shall receive one such little child in My name receiveth Me. But whoso shall offend one of these little ones which believe in Me, it were better for him that a millstone were hanged about his neck,*

and that he were drowned in the depth of the sea.
(Matthew 18:1-6)

This is serious business, isn't it? Paul, writing to the Church of Corinth, told them:

Brethren, be not children in understanding: howbeit in malice be ye children, but in understanding be men. (I Corinthians 14:20)

Children get angry just like we do. The difference is that they soon forget their anger. They don't harbor deep hurts. They forget so easily. *"In malice, be ye children."* What a powerful exhortation!

When I preached forgiveness to my congregation in every service week after week (until I had preached it about fifteen times in a row), some members, no doubt, grew weary of the subject and wondered if I was being very loving.

Yet, during that time nearly every member in my church discovered some area of unforgiveness in his/her life and was able to deal with it and go on to greater victories in God. Others felt releases in their spirits from nagging doubts and torments.

Many of them had been unaware that anything was wrong. They had locked their unforgiveness away in the deep recesses of their soul. But, thank God, He is a master computer operator. He knows how to access the most hidden parts of the soul. Nothing is hidden from His scrutiny. And He can bring to light what nobody else knows exists.

It is not unloving of the Lord to bring those things to light. We must not allow them to remain locked up in our spirits. For they will smother our souls; they will afflict our bodies; they will hinder our prayers; and they will delay our prosperity. It is a vicarious act of God's love that brings these hidden hurts and resentments to the surface to be dealt with. Don't resist Him in this. Welcome His intervention. Allow the Holy Ghost to probe the deep places of your soul. Don't leave any room of your heart unsearched and possibly unclean.

Many times love means confronting another brother to get the hurts out in the open and clarify things. It is not unloving to say, "Brother, something you did offended me, and I would like to clarify the situation so that we can be blessed." It is not unloving to say, "Sister, something you said offended me, and I want to clarify it so that we won't have any hindrance to our prayers." Love demands it.

Do it sooner rather than later. Do it now rather than tomorrow. Don't let the sun go down on this incident. Handle it wisely. Handle it with love. Forgive.

If that brother or sister has indeed done something to offend you, and if they repent and ask forgiveness, fine. If not, fine. Don't let anything or anyone keep you out of heaven. Forgive them, whatever their decision or attitude.

If Stephen could forgive people who were stoning him to death and Paul could forgive those who had beaten him and could sing God's praises in the prison at the midnight hour, you can do it too. This is the greatest love story ever told.

There is nothing wrong with praying that God will help those who have offended us to realize the error they have committed. We hope He will do that. But, if they refuse to heed His wooing, we will forgive anyway. Our spiritual welfare demands it.

Many of the people in our community and in our church have German backgrounds. Part of that hard German shell has been the concept of always being right and of hating to say, "I was wrong." That tradition has hindered many people. I have made many mistakes. You have too. Let us be ready and willing to recognize that fact, to ask God for forgiveness, to ask one another for forgiveness and to forgive those who have wronged us.

I refuse to harbor ill will in my spirit. I refuse to allow a root of bitterness to get hold of my life. I release every hurt, every disappointment, every ill will. It is the only way I can have complete victory in my life.

Believers often wonder what type of church they should attend. Should they look for a church that has a lot of good musical ability? Should their major concern be a church that has classes for every age level? There are many considerations to be made when looking for a good church. But of one thing I am sure: we should all be looking for a church that teaches love and forgiveness, a church free of pettiness and bickering. This is the spirit of Christ. Forgiveness is the Gospel in a nutshell. If we are forgiving, we are obeying the Gospel, we are living in the fulness of the Word of God.

It is so easy to hold grudges against people who have done us wrong, those who have cheated us out of money, those who have taken advantage of our kindness, those who have deceived us in some way. But, when we do, we are the losers. And we can't afford to do it. It makes no difference what the circumstances are. We must forgive.

> *Then said He unto the disciples, It is impossible but that offences will come: but woe unto him, through whom they come! It were better for him that a millstone were hanged about his neck, and he cast into the sea, than that he should offend one of these little ones. Take heed to yourselves: If thy brother trespass against thee, rebuke him; and if he repent, forgive him. And if he trespass against thee seven times in a day, and seven times in a day turn again to thee, saying, I repent; thou shalt forgive him. And the apostles said unto the Lord, Increase our faith.* (Luke 17:1-5)

"Rebuke" means "*to charge strictly.*" We are often quick to rebuke people who offend us, to charge them with something. We are quick to call others into judgment. We are quick to take action against those who offend us. But we are not quick to do the one thing we must do...forgive.

We always blame our problems on someone else. If you have ever visited the penitentiary, you know what I am talking about. Every man there is innocent (to hear them tell it). Very few of those imprisoned for serious crimes are willing to recognize their offenses. Most of them blame their incarceration on the mistakes of someone else.

"I was railroaded." "I was set up." "I was framed." "It's a bum rap." "It wasn't my fault." "All I was doing was holding a gun, nothing else." "I never intended to shoot nobody." "I didn't do it." If you listen to these men long enough, they will convince you that all the innocent people in the world are locked up, and the guilty people are running around free. They blame the arresting officers, the members of the jury, the judges, the defense attorneys, false witnesses, anyone and everyone, but themselves.

I know just how they feel. When I was a boy, in the seventh or eighth grade, my mother caught me smoking a cigarette. I thought she had gone back to work, and I was lying on the couch, sucking on a Lucky Strike. She had forgotten something, and I didn't hear her approaching on the concrete porch. When she opened the door and saw me, she was horrified.

"You're smoking!" she said.

"No! Mama, I ain't smokin'," I replied, trying vainly to lie to her. But I couldn't get the cigarette out quickly enough, and she knew the truth. I was mad at the cigarette, not at myself. Why couldn't that cigarette go out faster?

We don't want to admit our faults. We always blame someone else or something else. But, you are your own worst enemy. You are hurting yourself more than you are hurting anyone else. Forgive. Forgiveness is the greatest love story ever told.

Some people are hard to forgive. We all know people who are perpetually asking for forgiveness and perpetually repeating their offenses. "I promise," they swear, "I will never do that again." Usually they break their vow before the day is over. But the fact that they

frequently fail does not excuse us for holding something against them. If we do, we are the losers.

"My husband is forever doing this." "My wife continually does this." "My children do this and refuse to
change."

How can Jesus forgive such people? In His love, He
sees them through the eye of faith. He sees them as
they might be, as they should be. He doesn't see them
as they really are. And that's what you have to do when
you forgive. Start seeing that person through the eye of
faith. Believe for them to be that person they were destined to be. You don't know. This may be the time for
their change. Change your attitude toward that person, and they may change. Begin to project positive
statements toward that person rather than condemn-
ing them. You'll be surprised what God will do.

Stop saying: "My wife always does this," "My child
always does this,"or "My husband always does this."
Start seeing your husband in a different light, and
begin to say: "My husband has repented of the past.
He is a changed man. I receive his repentance, and I
have forgiven him. I refuse to see him in that old light.
I am determined to see him as the man that God says
he will be."

That is love in action, forgiving a person who sins
against you seven times in one day and believing for
their change. When Jesus required this of the disciples, they recognized the need for their faith to be increased. They said, *"Lord, Increase our faith."*

Forgiveness is a divine act, and without the faith
and love of God in our hearts we are incapable of the
level of forgiveness which the Lord requires of us. How

many of us have said, "I have taken so much, I simply can't take any more of it." And we mean it. There are definite limits to our power to forgive. We need more faith, more love of God, more anointing of the Holy Spirit. One of His gifts or manifestations in our lives is "*longsuffering*" (Galatians 5:22). Another of those gifts is "*love*" of which Paul taught the Corinthians:

Charity suffereth long, and is kind; charity envieth not; charity vaunteth not itself, is not puffed up. (I Corinthians 13:4)

It is not enough to say, "I forgive you," just as it is not enough to say, "I love you." Sometimes those are cheap words. These words must come from the heart and be accompanied by acts. We often tell people that we forgive them. Then, when they do something else to offend us, we throw up in their faces all the things we say we have already forgiven... showing that we haven't really done it. Some people can remember every detail of an offense that took place twenty years ago. That is not godly forgiveness. When God forgives, He also forgets.

In the Church, we have a problem with forgiving brothers and sisters who have sinned. But God doesn't have any such problem. He still considers them to be His children, and is more than happy to reinstate them to their place of privilege. His Word declares:

But if we walk in the light, as He is in the light, we have fellowship one with another, and the blood of Jesus Christ his Son cleanseth us from all sin. (I John 1:7)

When I become a child of God, the blood of Jesus Christ is applied to my sins, and I am forgiven. After that, if I sin, I may call upon God to forgive my sins. I haven't lost my relationship with God, but it may have been damaged, and I have almost certainly lost my fellowship. When I am willing to recognize my failure and to ask Him for forgiveness, He is faithful and just to forgive me and to restore me. Why can we not do the same for others?

Children can be very troublesome. They can betray your trust. They can take advantage of you. They can do terrible things. But, through it all, they are still our children, and if they are willing to repent of the things they have done and change, we are usually more than happy to treat them as we always have. Can God do less with His children? He places our transgression in the sea of forgetfulness and remembers it against us no more. We must do the same.

God's forgiveness is the greatest love story ever told. We have been forgiven. God's love, manifested through Christ on the cross of Calvary, has paid the price for our forgiveness. But, in order to receive that forgiveness, we must first forgive. Then, we must walk in forgiveness

It seems that everyone in the Church is looking for a "deep revelation." Well, this is about as deep as they come. When you begin to walk in total forgiveness, you will be walking in total love. And, because God is love, you will be walking with God. There could be no greater revelation. Forgiveness is the greatest love story ever told.

These were not easy lessons for the disciples to learn.

Then came Peter to him, and said, Lord, how oft shall my brother sin against me, and I forgive him? till seven times? Jesus saith unto him, I say not unto thee, Until seven times: but, Until seventy times seven. (Matthew 18:21-22)

Peter thought he was being generous when he suggested to Jesus that he might forgive a person up to seven times. He must have been as surprised as we are with Jesus' answer. Seven times is not enough, Jesus said. We should forgive *"seventy times seven." That's four hundred and ninety times and rather hard for us to fathom. Forgiveness is important.*

Jesus went on to tell the marvelous story of the forgiving king and the unforgiving servant, a story we will get to in Part III. Peter's understanding of this concept was very important. He would play a key role in the establishment of the Church. From the beginning, he had been part of an inner circle of believers. Jesus had special things for him.

When Jesus came into the coasts of Caesarea Philippi, He asked His disciples, saying, Whom do men say that I the Son of man am? And they said, Some say that Thou art John the Baptist: some, Elias; and others, Jeremias, or one of the prophets. He saith unto them, But whom say ye that I am? And Simon Peter answered and said, Thou art the Christ, the Son of the living God. And Jesus answered and said unto him, Blessed art thou, Simon-Barjona: for flesh and blood hath not revealed it unto thee, but my Father which is in heaven. And I say also unto thee, That thou art Peter, and upon this rock I will build My church; and the gates of hell shall not prevail against it. And I will give unto thee the keys of the kingdom of heaven: and whatsoever thou shalt bind on earth shall be bound in heaven: and whatsoever thou shalt loose on earth shall be loosed in heaven. (Matthew 16:13-19)

Peter was promised that he would receive *"the keys to the kingdom."* I am persuaded that those keys represented the power to forgive or not to forgive. Nothing binds like unforgiveness. And nothing looses like forgiveness.

After living a life of forgiveness and teaching His disciples to live in the same spirit, Jesus died a death of forgiveness.

And there were also two other, malefactors, led with Him to be put to death. And when they were come to the place, which is called Calvary, there they crucified Him, and the malefactors, one on the right hand, and the other on the left. Then said Jesus, Father, forgive them; for they know not what they do. And they parted His raiment, and cast lots. (Luke 23:32-34)

After all is said and done, Jesus is our example...not Moses or Joseph or Martin Luther or John Wesley, but Jesus. He had to be the first partaker. He had to be the firstfruits of everything that God would reveal to us. And Jesus forgave.

What would have happened if Jesus hadn't prayed this prayer? He couldn't have known the resurrection power of God without forgiving those who wronged Him. He could never have walked in a glorified body if He had not first learned to forgive. He could never have exercised power over satan and his legions of demons if He had not walked in forgiveness.

Because Jesus was forgiving, death could not keep Him. Hell could not prevent Him. The grave could not hold Him. He came forth victorious over every foe.

We must remember that Jesus was totally man while He was on the earth. He had to become flesh in order to take upon Himself our sins. He had to bear all that we bear. He had to be tempted in every point. He had to be touched with the feelings of our infirmities. He was very much a human with all the emotions and feelings associated with our human state.

When He was hanging on that cross, Jesus had every right to resent what was being done to Him. He didn't deserve that treatment. He had wronged no man. He had offended no one. He had broken no law. He had stolen no man's goods. He had violated no one's rights. He was innocent.

Yet, Jesus was wise enough to know that, although He had the "right" to be resentful and angry, He could not afford to harbor anything in His heart against anyone, even against His enemies. He released the whole matter into His Father's hands. *"Forgive them,"* He prayed. It was as easy as that. What more needed to be said about the matter. That ended it. Jesus forgave.

When that was done, Jesus could pray, *"It is finished."* Until you have forgiven every man, woman, boy and girl who has offended you, you have a lot of unfinished business. Get on with it. Let Jesus be your example. Forgive.

In this way, Jesus refused, even in death, to give place to the devil. He said, of satan: He "hath nothing in me."

Hereafter I will not talk much with you: for the prince of this world cometh, and hath nothing in me. (John 14:30)

Are you living the Christ-like life? Do you have Christ-like attitudes? Are you treating your friends, your family members, your neighbors and your associates in a Christ-like way?

Forgive. That is the CHRISTian way.

Jesus was sacrificed for my forgiveness, and He was sacrificed for your forgiveness. His blood was shed for the cleansing of our sin, our offenses. Through His supreme act of love we are forgiven.

Now, He is calling on us to reciprocate His love, to forgive the offenses of others. What are we waiting for? Let's do it today.

Part II

How Forgiveness Affects You Personally

Chapter 5

Forgiveness and Your Salvation

For if ye forgive men their trespasses, your heavenly Father will also forgive you: But if ye forgive not men their trespasses, neither will your Father forgive your trespasses. (Matthew 6:14-15)

So likewise shall My heavenly Father do also unto you, if ye from your hearts forgive not every one his brother their trespasses. (Matthew 18:35)

Your salvation does not depend upon how other people treat you. Initially, it depends entirely on your acceptance of the Lord Jesus Christ as your personal Savior. As you continue your Christian life, however, there is another element that can affect—for good or for bad—the welfare of your soul. Jesus clearly outlined it here. It is your willingness or unwillingness to reciprocate God's love and forgiveness, by extending that love and forgiveness to others.

When we come to the communion table, a reenactment of Calvary's sacrifice and its application to our

own hearts, this is one of the most important issues we
are to consider. Paul wrote to the Corinthians:

> *Wherefore whosoever shall eat this bread, and
> drink this cup of the Lord, unworthily, shall be
> guilty of the body and blood of the Lord. But let a
> man examine himself, and so let him eat of that
> bread, and drink of that cup. For he that eateth
> and drinketh unworthily, eateth and drinketh
> damnation to himself, not discerning the Lord's
> body. For this cause many are weak and sickly
> among you, and many sleep. For if we would
> judge ourselves, we should not be judged. But
> when we are judged, we are chastened of the
> Lord, that we should not be condemned with the
> world.* (I Corinthians 11:27-32)

What does it mean to partake of the communion
table *"unworthily?"* This is clearly an important question. The lack of discernment in this matter has led to
weakness and sickness among the members of the
Body of Christ and even to death (*"and many sleep"*).

The offense that leads to weakness, sickness and
death is described by Paul as *"not discerning the
Lord's body."* We understand that this refers not to the
emblems of the communion table, but to the mystical
Body of Christ, the fellowship of believers on the
earth. As we shall see in a later chapter, the unity of
brothers is one of God's top priorities.

Partaking of the communion *"unworthily,"* then,
may refer to partaking with unforgiven sin in our
lives, or it may refer to partaking with unforgiveness
in our hearts toward a brother, not discerning the importance of maintaining unity with our brothers,

refusing to extend to others what God has freely extended to us.

When we do partake of the communion in this way, that which was intended as blessing turns into cursing. We *eat and drink damnation.* Having seen the foundations of forgiveness and unforgiveness as powerful seeds that always produce a harvest, as the power to bind and loose, and as keys that lock and unlock the heavens to us, we can now understand why this is such a serious offense and why God cannot bless us when unforgiveness is present.

When you tie the hands of God, His precious blood is made of no effect in your personal life. He died for you. His atonement was accomplished for you. But His blood cannot be applied when your heart is full of unforgiveness toward others.

When we think of the possibility of losing our souls, we usually think of the sins of spiritual pride, adultery, or a lust for money or power. These are the sins that seem to overtake so many. Yet, simple things like anger and strife can be just as deadly and probably destroy as many as sins we consider to be much more serious. Paul wrote to the Ephesians:

That ye put off concerning the former conversation the old man, which is corrupt according to the deceitful lusts; And be renewed in the spirit of your mind; And that ye put on the new man, which after God is created in righteousness and true holiness. Wherefore putting away lying, speak every man truth with his neighbour: for we are members one of another. Be ye angry, and sin not:

let not the sun go down upon your wrath: Neither give place to the devil. (Ephesians 4:22-27)

God didn't say that we would never be angry. He said that we must not sin when we are angry. The anger itself may be justified. But the sin comes in when we refuse to forgive the person or persons who have made us angry.

Being angry is not the problem. Jesus was angry when He saw how the people of His day had profaned the Temple. It is normal to be angry by wrong doing. Being angry is not the problem. Not forgiving those who made you angry is the real problem. It is the unforgiveness that will poison your system. Don't let the sun go down before you have forgiven all those who have wronged you. The welfare of your soul demands it. This issue is just that important.

In the Sermon On The Mount, Jesus dealt with this issue, showing us clearly we must forgive so that we can keep the heavens open to our prayers. We must forgive so that we can be forgiven. We must forgive so that we can remain in God's blessing. If we fail to forgive, we cannot be forgiven. It could not be more clear.

When we ask God to forgive us for some offense against Him, it is for our sake, not His. Our sins don't cause God any problem. He can handle sin. He has been disappointed before. He doesn't harbor ill will against anyone. He is a loving and forgiving God. His mercy is fresh every morning. That is not to say that He approves of sin or is happy when we fail.

If we confess our sins, he is faithful and just to forgive us our sins, and to cleanse us from all unrighteousness. (I John 1:9)

There is a fine line here that many of us don't understand. In trying to convince the people of God not to walk in condemnation, sometimes we have given the impression that men can do whatever they want to do and prosper. And that simply is not so. God has called us to a life of holiness and righteousness.

The fact is, however, that we are all far from perfect. We fail and need God's forgiveness. Why, then, do we expect everyone else to be so perfect? And why do we hold it against them when they cannot live up to our high expectations?

It is this high and mighty attitude that puts us in trouble with God. He is ready and willing to forgive us when we err. He is ready and willing to lift us up when we stumble and fall. He cannot permit our unwillingness to extend this same mercy to others.

On the basis of this fact, I ask you: what is the sin that God cannot forgive? We have always asserted that only the sin of blasphemy cannot be forgiven. But, clearly, there is a second sin which cannot be forgiven. It is the sin of unforgiveness. If you cannot forgive others, God cannot forgive you.

Many other scriptures confirm this thought. Everything is possible with God but one. If you have unforgiveness in your heart, God cannot forgive you.

Therefore, with regularity, when we partake of the communion table, we must examine ourselves to see if evil seeds of hurt, resentment, and conflict have been sown in our hearts. What a shame it would be to live most of your adult life as a believer and then lose your soul because someone had offended you!

What are you waiting for? Forgive!

Chapter 6

Forgiveness and Your Healing

Is any sick among you? let him call for the elders of the church; and let them pray over him, anointing him with oil in the name of the Lord: And the prayer of faith shall save the sick, and the Lord shall raise him up; and if he have committed sins, they shall be forgiven him. Confess your faults one to another, and pray one for another, that ye may be healed. The effectual fervent prayer of a righteous man availeth much. (James 5:14-16)

What is it that we need to confess to someone so that we can be healed? Is it not unforgiveness? If you have committed adultery, you don't need to go tell other people about it. Tell the Lord. Don't contaminate other people's minds with your sin. But if you have wronged another person by harboring unforgiveness in your heart, this must be confessed to them personally. It is the sins against each other that must be confessed so that healing can take place.

Jesus showed a direct link between healing and forgiveness.

And, behold, they brought to Him a man sick of the palsy, lying on a bed: and Jesus seeing their faith said unto the sick of the palsy; Son, be of good cheer; thy sins be forgiven thee. And, behold, certain of the scribes said within themselves, This man blasphemeth. And Jesus knowing their thoughts said, Wherefore think ye evil in your hearts? For whether is easier, to say, Thy sins be forgiven thee; or to say, Arise, and walk? But that ye may know that the Son of man hath power on earth to forgive sins, (then saith He to the sick of the palsy,) Arise, take up thy bed, and go unto thine house. And he arose, and departed to his house. (Matthew 9:2-7)

Forgiveness is the first step in the healing process. You cannot be healed with unforgiveness in your heart—with jealousy in your heart, with bitterness in your heart, with strife in your heart.

I have experienced, at various times, problems in my body—aches and pains and sicknesses, and I didn't understand what was happening. In time, I learned that my physical suffering was due to some root of unforgiveness in my heart, and I was healed. So, I know what I am talking about. Many, if not all, of our sicknesses have their roots deep inside the recesses of our souls.

It was the power of forgiveness that raised this palsied man. And it is the power of unforgiveness that makes many people sick. Jesus' message to you today is, "Take up your bed and walk!" Just like this man in the story, you can have a clean slate in life. Just like this man, you can have a fresh start in life.

Many of the most crippling diseases known to man, among them: crippling arthritis, hypertension, and nervous disorders, have been directly traced to anxieties and stresses directly related to our inability to live at peace with one another. This is serious business.

You can't afford to hold grudges. You can't afford to keep bad thoughts in the back of your mind. You can't afford for tiny words, improper handshakes, unintended slights, or wrong looks to keep you from God's best for your life. What a husband does or a wife does or a child does or a friend does or an employer does or a co-worker does must not prevent you from attaining all of life's blessings. Don't let satan make you sick with worry and resentment.

If you have a loved one who has a prolonged sickness, a child, a husband or wife, a father or mother, and you have to spend all of your time taking care of that sick person, it can be devastating. It can rob you of your time and opportunity in life. It can overrule everything else in life and totally dominate you. This is serious. We need to learn what causes sickness and to nip it in the bud so that we can have victory in our lives. We want to solve all our problems with a national health policy, but that won't solve them. We need to forgive and be forgiven.

God's will for us is more than health and healing. Jesus gave us power to heal the sick and to cast out devils. In order to exercise that power, however, we need to walk in God's love and power. Relatively few believers are doing that today. What has happened to the power the disciples received on the Day of Pentecost? What has happened to our ability to put the devil in his place? Could unforgiveness be the root of our problem? I am convinced that it is.

Chapter 7

Forgiveness and Your Prosperity

But I say unto you, That whosoever is angry with his brother without a cause shall be in danger of the judgment: and whosoever shall say to his brother, Raca, shall be in danger of the council: but whosoever shall say, Thou fool, shall be in danger of hell fire. Therefore if thou bring thy gift to the altar, and there rememberest that thy brother hath ought against thee; Leave there thy gift before the altar, and go thy way; first be reconciled to thy brother, and then come and offer thy gift. (Matthew 5:22-24)

Does anger have something to do with your gifts to God and the blessings He has promised you in return? Does reconciliation have something to do with financial prosperity? Absolutely.

In this passage of the Sermon on the Mount, Jesus tells us that if we bring an offering to Him and have something in our hearts against a brother, He can't receive our offering. And if He can't receive our offering, He can't pour out on us the blessings promised in His Word regarding our giving.

He said it was better to *"leave"* our gift *"before the altar"* while we go and make things right with our brothers and sisters. Then, and only then, does He promise to honor our gifts.

The promises of God are great:

...your reward shall be great.... (Luke 6:35)

Give, and it shall be given unto you; good measure, pressed down, and shaken together, and running over, shall men give into your bosom. For with the same measure that ye mete withal it shall be measured to you again. (Luke 6:38)

Before you can have good measure, *"pressed down, shaken together and running over,"* you must learn to forgive. If you thought there was no connection between the two thoughts, it might be good for us to look at that entire passage more closely.

But I say unto you which hear, Love your enemies, do good to them which hate you, Bless them that curse you, and pray for them which despitefully use you. And unto him that smiteth thee on the one cheek offer also the other; and him that taketh away thy cloak forbid not to take thy coat also. Give to every man that asketh of thee; and of him that taketh away thy goods ask them not again. And as ye would that men should do to you, do ye also to them likewise. For if ye love them which love you, what thank have ye? for sinners also love those that love them. And if ye do good to them which do good to you, what thank have ye? for sinners also do even the same. And if ye lend to them of whom ye hope to receive, what thank have ye? for sinners also lend to sinners, to receive as much again. But love ye your enemies, and do good, and lend, hoping for nothing again; and your reward shall be great, and ye shall be the children of the Highest: for he is kind unto the unthankful and to the evil. Be ye therefore merciful, as your Father also is merciful. Judge not, and ye shall not be judged: condemn not, and ye shall not be condemned: forgive, and ye shall be forgiven: Give, and it shall be given unto you; good measure, pressed down, and shaken together, and running over, shall men give into your bosom. For with the same measure that ye mete withal it shall be measured to you again. (Luke 6:27-38)

Doesn't it seem odd that just before verse 38, that great message of faith and prosperity, comes verse 37, that great message of forgiveness? Could it be that forgiveness has something directly to do with men giving into your bosom, *"pressed down, shaken together, and running over?"* Of course it does. When you loose the hand of God over your life, you are going to get blessed in every way. And when you bind the hand of God you effectively prevent Him from blessing every area of your life.

Before you can have "good measure, pressed down, shaken together and running over," you must learn to forgive. The promise of prosperity is the culmination of a series of teachings which include such themes as: *Loving Your Enemies, Returning Good For Evil, and The Golden Rule.* Jesus showed us that we can't have the same attitude as the unsaved and expect to be blessed. He said:

For if ye love them which love you, what thank have ye? for sinners also love those that love them. And if ye do good to them which do good to you, what thank have ye? for sinners also do even the same. And if ye lend to them of whom ye hope to receive, what thank have ye? for sinners also lend to sinners, to receive as much again. But love ye your enemies, and do good, and lend, hoping for nothing again; and your reward shall be great, and ye shall be the children of the Highest: for he is kind unto the unthankful and to the evil. (Luke 6:32-35)

He concluded that section by saying:

Be ye therefore merciful, as your Father also is merciful. (Luke 6:36)

In order not to be judged, He told us not to judge.

In order not to be condemned, He told us not to condemn.

In order to be forgiven, He told us to forgive.

In order to receive, He told us to give.

And they are all intrinsically linked together. The blessing of prosperity comes with the willingness not to judge, the willingness not to condemn, and the willingness to forgive.

We must never forget the concluding words of Jesus:

For with the same measure that ye mete withal it shall be measured to you again. (Luke 6:38)

Never forget it—"with the same measure."

Perhaps something else needs to be said of prosperity to lend balance to our teaching. There is a "prosperity Gospel" and there is a Gospel that produces prosperity. And they are not the same. Some people are obsessed with financial gain—at the risk of losing their own soul. The Gospel that produces prosperity teaches that if we keep our souls right with God everything else will take care of itself.

Prosperity is wonderful when we maintain a godly life-style. But any blessing that draws us away from God and His best for our lives becomes a curse. It is possible to have a full bank account and still be miserable.

One of the churches that the Lord addressed in John's Revelation, the Church of Laodicea, was "rich and increased with goods." At the same time, however, it was "wretched and miserable."

Because thou sayest, I am rich, and increased with goods, and have need of nothing; and knowest not that thou art wretched, and miserable, and poor, and blind, and naked.... (Revelation 3:17)

The people of the Church of Laodicea, no doubt, thought they were doing well. They didn't realize how very miserable they were, until the Lord pointed it out. Riches are deceitful. They are not an end in themselves. They are only part of a larger picture of true prosperity for those who love and honor God.

Chapter 8

Forgiveness and Holy Ghost Power

And when the day of Pentecost was fully come, they were all with one accord in one place. And suddenly there came a sound from heaven as of a rushing mighty wind, and it filled all the house where they were sitting. And there appeared unto them cloven tongues like as of fire, and it sat upon each of them. And they were all filled with the Holy Ghost, and began to speak with other tongues, as the Spirit gave them utterance. (Acts 2:1-4)

Why did Holy Ghost power come on the Day of Pentecost? Because *"they were all with one accord."* There was an absence of hatred, malice and bitterness among the disciples of Jesus. That's what it takes. God blesses unity and reconciliation.

What do we need to do to get ready for a fresh Pentecost? We need to get rid of the things that have separated us from our brothers—hurts, disappointments, jealousies and misunderstandings.

When Holy Ghost power fell on the Day of Pentecost, it made those who received it powerful. When Peter began to preach that day, he was a changed man. He had been such a failure until then. Then, in one day, five thousand souls came to the feet of Jesus through his message.

And from the Day of Pentecost forward Peter was so powerful that even his shadow brought healing to those it passed over. He and the other disciples present in the Upper Room that day were able to bring healing to multitudes of people. The results of their ministry were the same as that of Jesus.

There came also a multitude out of the cities round about unto Jerusalem, bringing sick folks, and them which were vexed with unclean spirits: and they were healed every one. (Acts 5:16)

One morning, when Peter and John were on their way to the temple, a crippled man was sitting at the gate watching people go in and out and asking them for alms. The disciples had nothing of this world's goods to give him. But Peter said to the man, *"Such as I have give I thee: In the name of Jesus Christ of Nazareth rise up and walk"* (Acts 3:6). What did he have? He had God's miracle working power because he was walking in forgiveness. He had nothing in his heart against his brothers. He was living in harmony and blessing.

You can't do the works of God without power. You can't cast out demons without power. You can't heal the sick without power. You can't reach the lost without power. And that power doesn't come to those who live their lives in bitterness and resentment. It comes to those who are "with one accord."

God intended for His people to be powerful. He said that the gates of hell would not prevail against the true Church. But it is not enough to go through the motions of saying the right words or of laying hands on people, if the power of God is not present in our lives.

God intended for His people to stand strong against all the onslaught of the enemy. If we can't live for God now, in this present day and age, how will we stand in the evil times that are coming very shortly? World events are swirling toward a climax. It is wake-up time. You need God's power. If you know the Lord and are firmly planted in His love, you have nothing to fear. But if you are not squarely placed on that Solid Rock, you must wake up fast. Time is running out. The true Church must stand up and be seen in these last days. Jesus said that we would be known by our fruits.

Beware of false prophets, which come to you in sheep's clothing, but inwardly they are ravening wolves. Ye shall know them by their fruits. Do men gather grapes of thorns, or figs of thistles? Even so every good tree bringeth forth good fruit; but a corrupt tree bringeth forth evil fruit. A good tree cannot bring forth evil fruit, neither can a corrupt tree bring forth good fruit. Every tree that bringeth not forth good fruit is hewn down, and cast into the fire. Wherefore by their fruits ye shall know them. Not every one that saith unto Me, Lord, Lord, shall enter into the kingdom of heaven; but he that doeth the will of My Father

*which is in heaven. Many will say to Me in that
day, Lord, Lord, have we not prophesied in thy
name? and in Thy name have cast out devils?
and in Thy name done many wonderful works?
And then will I profess unto them, I never knew
you: depart from Me, ye that work iniquity.* (Matthew 7:15-23)

This is serious business. We need God's power in
order to produce fruit suitable for the Kingdom of God.

We teach the authority of the believer, but we don't
let our people know how much that authority depends
on walking in forgiveness. We teach that every
believer has authority over the devil, yet we fail to emphasize to our people how much that authority depends on walking in forgiveness. Without forgiveness,
you forfeit your spiritual authority and open yourself
up to satan's attacks. There is no authority without
forgiveness. There is no power without forgiveness.

Forgiveness is our greatest weapon of warfare.
Don't go into battle without it.

*For the weapons of our warfare are not carnal,
but mighty through God to the pulling down of
strong holds;* (II Corinthians 10:4)

One of the weapons of power we have used is praying in tongues. Few have realized, however, that you
can pray in tongues from now until Jesus comes, but it
won't do you any good—if you don't have forgiveness in
your heart. If you want Holy Ghost power, forgive.

Chapter 9

Forgiveness, Faith and Answered Prayer

Again I say unto you, That if two of you shall agree on earth as touching any thing that they shall ask, it shall be done for them of My Father which is in heaven. (Matthew 18:19)

The promise of Matthew 18:19 is as great as any in the Bible. It refers to "any thing" that we might ask and promises, "it shall be done for them." That is powerful. A similar promise is given in the Gospel of Mark.

Therefore I say unto you, What things soever ye desire, when ye pray, believe that ye receive them, and ye shall have them. (Mark 11:24)

At the same time we are reading this great promise, we are all aware that many believers pray and pray and pray and pray, and yet never seem to get the answer to their prayers. We have to ask ourselves why that is. Jesus said, "*Ye shall have them.*" The word "*them*" is not mysterious. It refers directly to "*what things soever ye desire.*"

There is the element of faith. He said, "*Believe that ye receive them, and ye shall have them.*" Based on this verse, many have believed and taught that the only thing necessary to have your prayers answered is faith. And faith is important, but there is something more here. This verse is followed by an "*and.*" The thoughts expressed here continue into the next verse.

> *And when ye stand praying, forgive, if ye have ought against any: that your Father also which is in heaven may forgive you your trespasses. But if ye do not forgive, neither will your Father which is in heaven forgive your trespasses.* (Mark 11:25-26)

The conclusion we can reach from this passage is that if we are not able or willing to forgive others, God cannot effectively answer our prayers. Unforgiveness is sin, and sin binds the hands of God on our behalf.

Many prayers are being hindered by unforgiveness. Many healings are being hindered by unforgiveness. The salvation of many is being hindered by unforgiveness. The prosperity of many is being hindered by unforgiveness.

What someone has done to you doesn't matter, but the attitude you take in the presence of God because of what someone has done to you matters a lot.

You can have faith for answered prayer, therefore, but if your heart is full of unforgiveness you cannot expect to receive what you are asking for. It is only when you have forgiven those who have trespassed against you that you can pray with full assurance that God hears you and will answer.

Jesus had begun this teaching with an admonition to faith:

> *And Jesus answering saith unto them, Have faith in God. For verily I say unto you, That whosoever shall say unto this mountain, Be thou removed, and be thou cast into the sea; and shall not doubt in his heart, but shall believe that those things which he saith shall come to pass; he shall have whatsoever he saith.* (Mark 11:22-23)

It might be easy to conclude (if you haven't read the rest of the teaching) that *"whosoever"* can pray prayers of faith and do acts of faith. But that is a mistaken concept. *"Whosoever"* cannot pray the prayer of faith. *"Whosoever"* cannot believe God for the desires of his/her heart. Many of God's promises are for a chosen few, those who are willing to obey God.

Many Christians are confessing with their mouth that their businesses will do well. And positive confession is a powerful force. But, you can confess all day, and, your heart is full of unforgiveness, there will be absolutely no fruit of your confession, however positive.

It is impossible to pray effectively if you are walking in unforgiveness. It is impossible to pray a prayer of agreement when you harbor grudges in your hearts toward a brother or sister.

I don't know about you, but I want to be blessed of God. I want to be able to be healed when I pray. I want to know that heaven is at attention when I need help.

Faith is important, but unless your prayer of faith is made from a forgiving heart, the Lord cannot answer you. Fasting is important, but if you fast with the wrong attitude, it becomes a useless work of the flesh. Forgiveness is a more important element of prayer than either faith or fasting.

The forgiveness element in prayer is so vital that Jesus incorporated it directly into the model prayer He taught His disciples.

And forgive us our debts, as we forgive our debtors. (Matthew 6:12)

The fasting element was dealt with separately. The faith element was dealt with separately. But forgiveness is an integral part of prayer. Without forgiveness prayer is ineffective and useless. God doesn't even hear the prayers of those who have not forgiven their brothers.

The exercise of faith, therefore, depends on forgiveness. If you are walking in forgiveness you can be a doer of the Word. If not, nothing will happen for you. Your unforgiveness binds heaven's blessings.

Surely all of us would like to have more faith. Faith is powerful. When we have faith, we can rest assured that God will do just what He has spoken. We know He will do it. And when we know something in our hearts, when we have that kind of faith, there is nothing that can change the outcome. All hell may break loose, but we will see what we are believing for. Nothing in this world and nothing out of this world can stop God's blessings—except our own unwillingness to forgive.

Unforgiveness always hinders our faith. When we allow little things to build up in our hearts over a period of years, things that people have said that offended us, things that people have done that offended us, slowly but surely the simplicity of our faith is compromised.

When Jesus had finished His teachings on forgiveness in Matthew 18, some wonderful things happened. When He moved, the people moved with Him. When He ministered, there was a response. And God responded from heaven. Multitudes were healed.

And it came to pass, that when Jesus had finished these sayings, He departed from Galilee, and came into the coasts of Judaea beyond Jordan; And great multitudes followed Him; and He healed them there. (Matthew 19:1-2)

There were, on the other hand, places where Jesus was unable to heal and bless, places where not one single miracle could be done. The meaning is clear. Forgiveness looses the mighty hand of God over His people.

With this background, we look again at James' teaching about prayer.

Confess your faults one to another, and pray one for another, that ye may be healed. The effectual fervent prayer of a righteous man availeth much. (James 5:16)

Who is this "righteous man?" Righteousness is right standing, right thinking, and right acting. God has promised to answer the prayer of such a person. This verse makes it clear that a righteous person is one who has confessed any bad thoughts and feelings he may have harbored against another individual and has prayed for that person. This is the prayer God has promised to honor.

We have been reconciled to God through the precious blood of Jesus Christ. Now, we must be reconciled to each other. Forgive.

Chapter 10

Forgiveness and Unity Among Brothers

I Therefore, the prisoner of the Lord, beseech you that ye walk worthy of the vocation wherewith ye are called, With all lowliness and meekness, with longsuffering, forbearing one another in love; Endeavouring to keep the unity of the Spirit in the bond of peace. (Ephesians 4:1-3)

"Unity" refers to *"agreement,"* to being *"at one."* If we are to reach spiritual maturity and to do the work of the ministry, we must learn the secret of unity. I know people who have been in the faith for thirty years or more, and many would consider them to be mature. But they have no unity; and, without unity, there is no real power.

As we have seen, the disciples received power with the coming of the Holy Ghost on the Day of Pentecost because they were all *"with one accord"* (Acts 1:14 & 2:1). Unity brings power. A house divided is weak.

Solomon, in his wisdom, recognized this truth:

A threefold cord is not quickly broken. (Ecclesiastes 4:12)

If you have three separate strands and you weave them together, you still have the same three strands. They haven't changed. Separately they are still limited by the strength of each individual strand. But when those three strands are woven together, something wonderful happens. Together they take on a new strength and are not easily broken. There is a powerful truth here that we need to comprehend.

Did you ever hear of a one-man baseball team? How about a one-man basketball team? Is it possible to have a one-man football team? No. Each of these sports requires a team made up of various players—nine, five, or eleven, as the case may be. But in sports, as in other aspects of life, the various players of the team must learn to work together. They must agree together for a common goal and work together in unity to achieve that goal. Only then do they begin to win games.

The Bible likens the coordination of the physical body to the manner in which the Christian ministry should work.

For the body is not one member, but many. If the foot shall say, Because I am not the hand, I am not of the body; is it therefore not of the body? And if the ear shall say, Because I am not the eye, I am not of the body; is it therefore not of the body? If the whole body were an eye, where were the hearing? If the whole were hearing, where were the smelling? But now hath God set the members every one of them in the body, as it hath pleased him. (I Corinthians 12:14-18)

If your hand would try to do the work of your foot, you would be in trouble. The hand is not made for the work of the foot. If your ear would insist on doing the seeing, you would be in trouble. It's not made for that. But every member of the body accepts its role and does not work against the other parts. The various members all work together in harmony for the common good.

The Lord is waiting for the members of His Body to stop acting out of jealousy for one another and to start being "at one," in unity. This was the prayer of Jesus for us.

And now I am no more in the world, but these are in the world, and I come to thee. Holy Father, keep through Thine own name those whom Thou hast given Me, that they may be one, as We are. (John 17:11)

God is one. Although He has chosen to manifest Himself in three persons—God the Father, God the Son and God the Holy Ghost—He is one.

But to us there is but one God, the Father, of whom are all things, and we in Him; and one Lord Jesus Christ, by Whom are all things, and we by Him. (I Corinthians 8:6)

One Lord, one faith, one baptism. (Ephesians 4:5)

Can you imagine Jesus being jealous of the Holy Ghost and trying to gain the ascendancy over Him? Of course not. Well, we are created in His image. We, therefore, should strive for unity among ourselves.

> *For the perfecting of the saints, for the work of the ministry, for the edifying of the body of Christ: Till we all come in the unity of the faith, and of the knowledge of the Son of God, unto a perfect man, unto the measure of the stature of the fulness of Christ....* (Ephesians 4:12-13)

This *"perfecting"* refers to reaching maturity. Christ is mature, but His body has not yet reached maturity. He was one with His Father and with the Holy Ghost. We are still struggling to be one with the other members of our body. And this struggle is hindering the free exercise of the power destined to be ours through the Holy Ghost.

Webster defines unity as: *"The state of being one; the quality or fact of being totally whole; something complete in itself, one in purpose, an arrangement of parts or materials that will produce a single."*

If all the parts of a body are in the right arrangement, they produce a unified body, as happened on the Day of Pentecost. Because the disciples were united, were *"with one accord,"* they became powerful witnesses for the Lord Jesus Christ.

What does unity have to do with forgiveness and unforgiveness? Well, forgiveness brings unity, and unforgiveness brings division.

The disciples didn't know when the outpouring of the Holy Spirit would take place. They couldn't time their unity for a specific moment. They had to stay in unity. We don't know when God wants to do something special for us. Our blessing will come suddenly and unexpectedly, as did theirs.

When they got in unity, things happened quickly. They didn't have long to wait. God moves when we get united.

That the Body is one and yet has many members is a miracle. That can only happen when all the members are in unity, in agreement. When my body is working in agreement, I can carry out all the instructions my brain sends out to the other members of the body. As a spiritual body, God is our head; and since He is our head, we have no limitations.

It is when we come together in unity that all things are possible to us. One person walking in unforgiveness can hinder the whole body. One sore toe can affect the entire body. If you have ever had any problems with your toes, you know what I am talking about. One sore finger can cause suffering throughout the body.

All of the parts of the Body, all the various ministries are placed in the Body for our good, for the perfecting of the saints. For the body to be functioning properly, the arm must do its job. The shoulder must be in good condition and be properly functioning. The hand must be in its proper place and be properly functioning.

Even a hand, as useful as it is, cannot help itself. It takes another hand to help it. It takes all of us working together to make the Body of Christ function properly. You are not complete without me, and I am not complete without you. We need every member and every ministry working together to accomplish the task at hand.

No man is an island. God has called us to minister to each other. When one of your fingers is hurt, blood from all over your body rushes to that finger. The healing process starts working in every part of the body. If that finger rejects the help coming from the rest of the body, infection will set in and the finger will eventually be destroyed. When that happens, the offending part may sometimes have to be severed.

Christ is our example. He is one, but He also has several members.

> *For we are members of His body, of His flesh, and of His bones. For this cause shall a man leave his father and mother, and shall be joined unto his wife, and they two shall be one flesh. This is a great mystery: but I speak concerning Christ and the church.* (Ephesians 5:30-32)

The Church is to have a unity similar to that attained by the union of husband and wife in marriage. This is indeed a mystery!

We are destined to unity, and God has given us the ministries we need to grow into that unity. When we reach the maturity for which we are destined, there are many benefits. Each member helps the other.

What can my foot do? Can I use it to scratch my back? Can I use it to eat my food? Can I use it to brush my teeth? What can it do? Well, it can do a lot of things. But there are many other things that it cannot do. My foot, for instance, cannot reach up to brush my teeth. And, besides, I would have great difficulty holding the toothbrush with one of my feet.

One member cannot automatically replace another member. Each member is unique. Don't write off anyone as useless or unnecessary. Don't dismiss anyone as being unimportant or unessential.

We need the prophet. We need the apostle. We need the evangelist. We need the teacher. We need the pastor. Don't write any of these ministries off as "for another age." They are all for us, and we need them all.

In the beginning of this chapter of Paul's letter and at the ending of this chapter God is dealing with us about spiritual gifts. He is telling us that these gifts need to operate within an atmosphere of unity and for the common good. It is time to stop playing with these precious gifts and to start using them as it would please the Lord. Here is His will for the Body:

> *That there should be no schism in the body; but that the members should have the same care one for another. And whether one member suffer, all the members suffer with it; or one member be honoured, all the members rejoice with it.*
> (I Corinthians 12:25-26)

God wants a mature Body into which He can place His many gifts and manifestations for the benefit of everyone involved. This can only happen when we are in unity. And unity comes by forgiving one another and loving one another, as we are. If we profess love for God and do not love one another, we are deceiving ourselves.

> *If a man say, I love God, and hateth his brother, he is a liar: for he that loveth not his brother*

*whom he hath seen, how can he love God whom
he hath not seen?* (I John 4:20)

If part of your body offends you, if you break your
arm, for instance, you don't chop it off. You try to
protect it so that it has time to heal. Being vindictive
with your own arm cannot do any good for your body.

And the healing of a broken arm takes time. Even
when the cast comes off, we can't immediately do all
the things we once did. It takes time to make that
member work properly again. But we must have
patience with a weak part of the body, until it mends
and can carry its own weight. In the same way, we
need to be more loving and tender with those members
of the Body of Christ who are injured. It takes time for
them to be fully restored.

The 5th chapter of Paul's letter to the Galatians
ends in this way:

*Let us not be desirous of vain glory, provoking
one another, envying one another.* (Galatians 5:26)

Then, his theme seems to change abruptly, almost
like a train switching tracks.

*Brethren, if a man be overtaken in a fault, ye
which are spiritual, restore such an one in the
spirit of meekness; considering thyself, lest thou
also be tempted.* (Galatians 6:1)

But has Paul changed themes? Not at all. The way
to avoid the frictions mentioned in chapter 5 is to take
the loving action mentioned in chapter 6. Cutting off a
member of our own body is self defeating and foolish.

When we are reconciled to God, we want to work for the reconciliation of others. It doesn't matter what a brother has done, we are admonished to work toward his restoration.

That doesn't mean that we condone sin. We don't sit back idly when we know that our brothers have erred. But, what we do for them, is not done with a spiteful spirit or in revenge or as a grudge for some wrong they have done us. We work, rather, toward their reconciliation.

We are not called to go around pointing our fingers at our brothers and sisters. We are called to lift them up, to bear their burdens.

Bear ye one another's burdens, and so fulfil the law of Christ. (Galatians 6:2)

In the church today, we seem to be like little children running around a track in bumper cars, everyone working against everyone else, almost enjoying bouncing off each other in the process. It is time to grow up.

One of the greatest offenders is gossip, idle talk, talebearing, and rumor mongering. It is impossible to maintain harmony in the Body of Christ and participate in these demonic activities. Jesus said:

But I say unto you, That every idle word that men shall speak, they shall give account thereof in the day of judgment. (Matthew 12:36)

This phrase "every idle word" cannot refer to something as innocent as talking about the weather or about sports, new car models or clothes. God isn't offended when you talk about the weather. He is not upset when you talk about football. What offends God is when you speak against your brother.

The words of a talebearer are as wounds, and they go down into the innermost parts of the belly. (Proverbs 18:8)

He that covereth a transgression seeketh love; but he that repeateth a matter separateth very friends. (Proverbs 17:9)

These are serious sins against the Body of Christ that will not go unpunished. Why should anyone want to involve themselves in another person's affairs? Don't we each have enough trouble of our own without getting our noses into other people's affairs?

Where no wood is, there the fire goeth out: so where there is no talebearer, the strife ceaseth. (Proverbs 26:20)

These are powerful words that cut right to the heart of our present reality. Solomon received great wisdom from God to write these things thousands of years ago. Yet, it is like reading today's newspaper. Men haven't changed much.

As coals are to burning coals, and wood to fire; so is a contentious man to kindle strife. The words of a talebearer are as wounds, and they go down into the innermost parts of the belly. (Proverbs 26:21-22)

When those *"words of a talebearer"* *"go down into the innermost parts of the belly,"* they can take root and grow. We mustn't let that happen. We must be careful to deal with the hurts, wounds, and the disappointments of life, without slandering the lives of those around us. May God protect our lips from gossip and talebearing.

Gossip, such a simple word! Yet, gossip has the potential of doing great damage to the Body of Christ on the earth.

Some of us have a wrong concept concerning unity among brothers. We think that unity means we have to agree 100% on everything. It doesn't. Nobody in the world agrees with me 100%. We are all different. Nobody else thinks exactly as I do. Husbands and wives have disagreements. To be in unity doesn't mean that we agree on every point. That isn't possible. Each of us sees things from the perspective of our particular experience. And, the way we see things changes as time goes on.

Unity is not agreement on every point of belief. It goes far beyond that. In Christ, we are able to love each other and work together, despite the fact that we are so different. In the same way, the members of my physical body are very different. Yet they all work together toward a common goal and all benefit.

I cannot despise you because you see things a little differently than I do. As the physical body has unity in diversity, you and I can love each other—despite our differences. And if we remain united, satan can never get the advantage over us.

It is interesting to watch opposing lawyers at work on a legal case. They argue their case so strenuously. Then, when they have finished making their argument, then walk out the door of the court room and take each other to lunch. Christians ought to be that smart. Some Christians never speak to each other again once they have a disagreement over some minor point of doctrine.

Forgive!

Chapter 11

Forgiveness and
Unity in the Home

Can two walk together, except they be agreed?
(Amos 3:3)

God has ordained unity for husband and wife. He declares that He has made them *"one flesh"* (Matthew 19:5). This unity that God has ordained for spouses, however, doesn't happen through the mere union of the flesh. It happens only when both husband and wife get the mind of Christ and begin to think His thoughts. When they do, satan loses his power over that couple.

On the other hand, when there is constant disharmony in the home, satan gains a right to rule over that household, and there is absolutely nothing you can do about it. If you give him the advantage, he will take it every time.

How does the unity of the marriage break down? It doesn't happen over night. It may begin with a lack of unity in purpose. But that lack of unity in purpose may allow the growth of influences that threaten our well being. It may begin with a misunderstanding. But misunderstandings usually breed disappointment, anger, resentment and strife. And, as things take their natural course, the results can be devastating.

Marriage partners have the potential to hurt each other as no one else can. Opening ourselves up to the most intimate relationships has its dangers as well as its benefits. This explains why people who begin loving each other so much can end up hating each other so much. And it all begins with some unforgiven deed or word. In the end, it is far from simple. It is very complicated.

"I trusted you. Why have you ruined my life?"

"I gave you everything. Why have you betrayed me?"

Sometimes we don't speak, but we also don't forgive. We keep our feelings inside, covered up, until they grow into major sticking points that often cause us severe damage.

Husbands and wives are particularly susceptible to the growth of resentment because they learn to know each other so well. When you get to know someone, you get to know not just the surface person, but you see the person with all their warts (so to speak), all their weaknesses and failures. If you want to avoid this problem, never get married. The only candidates for marriage are human, and all humans have weaknesses and failures.

When you get married, you have to be ready to accept some human frailties and to forgive them. If not you will destroy each other. Maybe you're perfect. If so, you're the only one, so you should remain single. You won't find a suitable mate.

It pains me to tell you, but I am not perfect either. Once my wife, Myrna, said to me, "You don't realize what a sharp tongue you have. Some of the things you say can cut to the heart." And I knew she was right. Husbands and wives have the potential to wound each other terribly. Thank God that my wife is a forgiving person. If she was looking for a perfect man, I have been a terrible disappointment. I am very human.

One night when I was preaching, I felt led to turn to her and ask her to forgive me for the little things I had said through the years that had hurt her. They meant nothing to me. I didn't even remember them, but I had offended her. As shepherds of the flock, we pastors must lead the way in repentance and forgiveness.

In most marriages, there are certain issues which we avoid discussing because each time we bring them up, it causes an argument. So we let them lie buried beneath the surface. We have a lot of burrs under our saddles, a lot of built up animosity just waiting its chance to burst to the surface and explode.

In your marriage, you certainly have a right to your opinion. You certainly are wronged at times by your mate. Fortunately, there is only one rule that you need to follow. Forgive, whatever the offense. Forgive, regardless of who is right and who is wrong. Forgive, regardless of who started the whole thing. Just forgive and forget.

Forget about your rights and start being concerned about your blessings. The source of your blessings is not your own ego, it is Almighty God. If your ego gets bruised a little, you'll survive. If your blessings get cut off, you won't. It's that simple.

Some resentments may be so deeply hidden that you don't recognize them any longer. Ask God to reveal them to you. He will. You don't need the intervention of a neighbor. You don't need to call on your pastor. Ask God to deal with your heart. No one can do it like He can.

Sometimes wounds heal on the surface but remain deadly under the skin. When this happens, the wound must be opened and dealt with or it will cause serious damage to the body. Proper healing begins on the inside and works it way out.

Some people have wounds that have seared over years ago and appear to be healed. But inside, they are festering sores that continue to torment those who received them. Many women who were molested in childhood or youth have never dealt with the festering sores that torment their souls. Those wounded areas have been covered and hidden, but they are still bubbling beneath the surface.

When husbands try to approach these women, they often draw back. This is mysterious to the husbands, who often have been told nothing of the sore place. Unless these women can forgive those who have so wronged them, they will never have the healthy and happy marital relationship they were destined to have. Open those sores and let them heal properly.

Similarly, there are broken relationships between father and child, and between brothers and sisters that need to be healed.

Another reason that spouses often offend each other is simply the ease of doing it. Because of the amount of time married people spend together and because of the intimacy of their relationship, they find it easy to confront each other, easy to rebuke each other, easy to insult each other. Husbands and wives often sin against each other in this way.

Some people are not quick to forgive. They want to make you suffer for a while and teach you a lesson. In the meantime, they are the ones who are suffering because of it, and they don't even know it. Unforgiveness will eat you up, physically and emotionally. It will cause you all kinds of complications.

Many divorced people are unsuccessful in their second marriages as well. They take into that second marriage all the unforgiveness that resulted from the failure of the first marriage. How can they prosper?

If you leave one job with bitterness and resentment, those feelings will follow you to the next job and keep you from being successful there too.

Some people bounce from one relationship to the next, from one job to the next, from one church to the next, never understanding why they can't make a go of anything. Why is it that some people can't make and keep friends? Why is it that some people can't get along with anybody? To me, the answer is easy. These people are so full of unforgiveness that they are like ticking time bombs, accidents waiting to happen.

Some people never recover from a divorce. They bear that hurt, that resentment, that bitterness to their graves. Well, divorce is never pleasant. But God wants to give you victory over EVERY hurt, and over EVERY resentment, and over EVERY bitterness. Don't allow the wrong that another person has done you keep you from the best of God's blessing upon the rest of your life. What affects us counts not only for the rest of our physical lives but also for all eternity.

If you are miserable, you make everyone else miserable. If you are bitter, you make everyone else bitter. Bitterness is a deadly cancer. Resentment is a deadly cancer. Unforgiveness is a deadly cancer. It will destroy you. And, in the process, the stench of it, the filth of it, the misery of it, will destroy many other people.

Why is it that the hardest words in the English language for many of us to utter is that simple refrain: I AM SORRY? Is that going to kill you to say that? I don't think so. Yet, some grown men, of forty or fifty years old or more, have never uttered the words. They would rather lose everything than humble themselves and admit that they made a mistake.

To these proud people, saying you are sorry is a sign of weaknesses. But they are wrong! Dead wrong! Saying "I'm sorry" is not a sign of weakness; it is a sign of strength and wisdom. The Bible says:

> *For godly sorrow worketh repentance to salvation not to be repented of: but the sorrow of the world worketh death.* (II Corinthians)7:10

Why is it so hard to say you are sorry? I believe it is because satan knows the power of those words and fights their use. Those are healing words. Those are blessing words.

Satan makes them difficult for us to say because he doesn't want us to have the key to the kingdom, the key to the heart of God.

Why has society developed the image of the macho man? Just like most everything else in our society, this is developed to keep us from God's best for our lives.

Husbands sometimes feel that if they admit they made a mistake, they are less of a man for it. They feel that if they admit they are wrong they are losing control. Isn't this ridiculous! Satan has deceived us into fearing to do the very thing we must do to get victory. Being humble, repentant and forgiving can unlock all the bolted doors in your household.

People in positions of authority in business think they have to project a "toughness" in order to gain respect. And, in doing so, they end up losing the respect of everyone around them.

Pride is a terrible thing. It keeps us from repenting of our wrongs and keeps us from forgiving others. Manly pride. Family pride. Professional pride. It's all bad. Pride is of the flesh, not of the Spirit.

When our children wrong each other, we want them to ask forgiveness, but we are not setting the example for them. We don't want to ask forgiveness ourselves. If you are wondering why it is so hard to get your child to say, "I'm sorry," you might find the answer in your own heart.

And when we do apologize, let's be sure that our "I'm sorry" is from the heart. It sometimes isn't. God knows. Like some others of the most important phrases known to man, this one can be misused. "I love you" can become a phrase of deception. Don't make "I'm sorry" a common phrase said without real meaning or change.

Through forgiveness, we keep an open heaven, and through repentance and forgiveness in the home, we keep open our channels of communication and respect. When we disobey God in the matter of forgiveness, satan is given an advantage over our household, a toe hold in our spiritual lives, a door of opportunity. And if a man or woman insists on living with a heart full of unrepented anger, jealousy, or hurt, God is powerless to prevent satan from doing what he will in that home. That person has effectively bound the hands of God on their own behalf.

Husbands, hear me. Wives, hear me. If your household is divided, you can't stand. You need God's favor upon your life. You can't exist without Him. You can't afford to live in constant resentment and misunderstanding. When Paul said, *"Neither give place to the devil,"* he was talking to you. If you don't open the door to him, he has no right to invade your home. If you keep your door sealed, he cannot exercise authority over you. The words, *"Don't let the sun go down on your wrath"* has no greater application than in the marriage and in the home, and that is where we most often fail to heed his warning. In so doing, we are opening the door to satan and his works. And, if we can't forgive the people we love, those with whom we live daily, how can we expect to have the proper attitude toward neighbors and even strangers?

Give satan no place in your life. Forgive.

Part III

Bible Characters and Forgiveness

Chapter 12

Jacob and Esau
and Forgiveness

Follow peace with all men, and holiness, without which no man shall see the Lord: Looking diligently lest any man fail of the grace of God; lest any root of bitterness springing up trouble you, and thereby many be defiled; Lest there be any fornicator, or profane person, as Esau, who for one morsel of meat sold his birthright. For ye know how that afterward, when he would have inherited the blessing, he was rejected: for he found no place of repentance, though he sought it carefully with tears. (Hebrews 12:14-17)

What a terrible way to be remembered in the Bible! Esau is remembered as a *"profane person,"* one who sought a place of repentance *"with tears,"* but could not find it. What a terrible legacy!

There is a further mystery in Scripture concerning these two brothers. God said of them:

Jacob have I loved, but Esau have I hated. (Romans 9:13)

*I have loved you, saith the Lord. Yet ye say,
Wherein hast Thou loved us? Was not Esau
Jacob's brother? saith the Lord: yet I loved Ja-
cob, and I hated Esau....* (Malachi 1:2-3)

These are very unusual passages in the Scriptures
and, as such, merit further investigation. God is not in
the hating business. He is a God of love. In fact, *"God
is love"* (I John 4:16).

What was it that God hated about Esau? And what
was it that He loved about Jacob? If Esau was a
"profane person," was Jacob any better? He was far
from perfect. Everyone knew what he was like. They
called him the *"supplanter,"* the *"deceiver."* He deceived his brother. He deceived his father, Isaac. He
stole the birthright from Esau. Was he any better than
Esau? And why was Esau a *"profane person?"* To get
the answers, we must look to Genesis.

*And these are the generations of Isaac,
Abraham's son: Abraham begat Isaac: And Isaac
was forty years old when he took Rebekah to wife,
the daughter of Bethuel the Syrian of Padan-
aram, the sister to Laban the Syrian. And Isaac
intreated the Lord for his wife, because she was
barren: and the Lord was intreated of him, and
Rebekah his wife conceived. And the children
struggled together within her; and she said, If it
be so, why am I thus? And she went to inquire of
the Lord. And the Lord said unto her, Two na-
tions are in thy womb, and two manner of people
shall be separated from thy bowels; and the one
people shall be stronger than the other people;*

and the elder shall serve the younger. And when her days to be delivered were fulfilled, behold, there were twins in her womb. And the first came out red, all over like an hairy garment; and they called his name Esau. And after that came his brother out, and his hand took hold on Esau's heel; and his name was called Jacob: and Isaac was threescore years old when she bare them. And the boys grew: and Esau was a cunning hunter, a man of the field; and Jacob was a plain man, dwelling in tents. And Isaac loved Esau, because he did eat of his venison: but Rebekah loved Jacob. (Genesis 25:19-28)

Isaac was sixty years old when his sons, Jacob and Esau, were born. Esau, when he grew up, became "*a cunning hunter.*" He was a man's man. If he were living today, we might call him a "jock." He loved to hunt and fish and to play sports. He would have been good at tennis. He would have loved to participate in the rodeo. He was a rugged outdoorsman. Because of this, Isaac preferred Esau.

This doesn't mean that Jacob didn't like sports or the out of doors. But what was noticeable about Jacob was that he had a heart toward God. He loved to sit at his mother's feet and hear the stories of Israel's exploits. He thrilled to hear of the promises of God to Abraham, his grandfather.

Rebecca was not surprised by this. God had already told her that the elder would serve the younger. She knew that something unusual would happen with these brothers, that they would not follow the course proscribed by society. She understood that Jacob was destined to blessing, while Esau would settle for mediocrity.

Jacob was far from perfect. His failings were obvious to anyone who wanted to look. And they didn't have to look very hard. But he looked into the spiritual world and caught a glimpse of the blessings of God that were coming his way, and he would not be denied. We may not approve of his methods, but we must applaud his vision.

Esau couldn't see the spiritual realm at all. He was too busy with his many physical activities. He was too busy "enjoying life." But while Esau was out "enjoying life," Jacob was learning more about the things of God. He believed the promise God had given to his mother at his birth. And throughout life he would not stray from the principles outlined by his mother in his childhood. Mothers have a great responsibility toward their children.

The line of inheritance would change with Jacob. The proper genealogy would have been Abraham, Isaac, and Esau. But it didn't work out that way. Esau lost his place because he despised the spiritual world. He despised his birthright. He thought he had found something better than what God promised to Abraham. He sold his blessing for something good to eat.

And Jacob sod pottage: and Esau came from the field, and he was faint: And Esau said to Jacob, Feed me, I pray thee, with that same red pottage; for I am faint: therefore was his name called Edom. And Jacob said, Sell me this day thy birthright. And Esau said, Behold, I am at the point to die: and what profit shall this birthright do to me? And Jacob said, Swear to me this day; and he sware unto him: and he sold his birthright unto Jacob. Then Jacob gave Esau bread and pottage of lentiles; and he did eat and drink, and rose up, and went his way: thus Esau despised his birthright. (Genesis 25:29-34)

Esau had no respect for the value of his birthright. It didn't mean much to him. He had other, more important, things to think about. I don't know what he had done that day that made him so hungry. Maybe he played a double-header that day. Maybe he pitched or caught a big game. Maybe he was a tailback who ran for record yardage. Or maybe he was a forward on the basketball team who scored big that day. Maybe he had run the mile or roped a calf. I don't know. Something made him awfully hungry. And he felt like eating was the most important thing he had to do right then. And Jacob knew how to take advantage of the situation. He was ready to feed his brother, but he wanted the birthright in return.

Was the birthright important? It represented a physical inheritance. But, most of all, it represented a spiritual inheritance, the line of blessing that was destined for the firstborn.

To Esau, however, the birthright was less than nothing—at that moment. He had no respect for it at all. He had carved out for himself a "better life." He would not be limited by the old fashioned, out-of-date concepts of his parents and grandparents. He was going to enjoy life as it was meant to be enjoyed.

To me, it is easy to see what God hated in Esau. He hated his disrespect. Esau had no respect for God; he had no respect for his forefathers and their faith; he had no respect for the promise; and he had no respect for his heritage. He said, "What profit shall this birthright do to me?"

Was Esau really starving to death? Did one good day in the field so exhaust him that food was all he could think about? I don't think so. I think he was a man who had his priorities all mixed up.

Esau would, or course, live to regret his hasty decision that day. His loss began to dawn on him the day his father blessed Jacob instead of him.

And when Esau heard the words of his father, he cried with a great and exceeding bitter cry, and said unto his father, Bless me, even me also, O my father. And he said, Thy brother came with subtilty, and hath taken away thy blessing. And he said, Is not he rightly named Jacob? for he hath supplanted me these two times: he took away my birthright; and, behold, now he hath taken away my blessing. And he said, Hast thou not reserved a blessing for me? And Isaac answered and said unto Esau, Behold, I have made him thy lord, and all his brethren have I given to him for servants; and with corn and wine have I sustained him: and what shall I do now unto thee, my son? And Esau said unto his father, Hast thou but one blessing, my father? bless me, even me also, O my father. And Esau lifted up his voice, and wept. (Genesis 27:34-38)

We always appreciate something once we have lost it. Esau *"lifted up his voice, and wept."* But did he do the right thing, even then? He blamed everything on Jacob. The problem, in his eyes, was Jacob's deceit, not his own lack of spirituality. He sold his birthright, then blamed his brother for stealing it.

Jacob understood the importance of the blessing that had belonged to Abraham. Evidently his mother had taught him well. But surely Rebecca had made an effort to teach Esau the things of God, as well. Surely she would not be guilty of showing favoritism in this regard. I believe she taught both boys equally, but Esau was not interested. One boy received and one boy rejected. It is as simple as that. That is why God could say that He loved Jacob, but hated Esau.

When it was already too late, Esau recognized what he was losing, and he wept and pleaded with his father to help him. Isaac loved Esau and was, no doubt, deeply moved by this incident. He would have wanted to bless the son he loved. But there was not much left. Jacob had received the major blessings. Isaac did what he could:

> *And Isaac his father answered and said unto him, Behold, thy dwelling shall be the fatness of the earth, and of the dew of heaven from above; And by thy sword shalt thou live, and shalt serve thy brother; and it shall come to pass when thou shalt have the dominion, that thou shalt break his yoke from off thy neck.And Esau hated Jacob because of the blessing wherewith his father blessed him: and Esau said in his heart, The*

*days of mourning for my father are at hand; then
will I slay my brother Jacob.* (Genesis 27:39-41)

Was Esau's "repentance" sincere? Did he ever
recognize his own lack? Apparently not, for when a
man sincerely repents, God hears his plea. Instead,
Esau went on living his life in bitterness, angry because he was sure his brother had robbed him of the
best life has to offer.

Jacob fled for his life and lived in exile for many
years. When the two brothers met once again, Esau
did forgive Jacob; and they were reconciled. But, even
then, was Esau sincere? The Edomites, as Esau's descendants came to be called, were a war-like people.
They lived in constant anger and frustration. They
could not know peace because they had never truly
forgiven.

How many people live in spiritual poverty because
they cannot bring themselves to forgive a brother, a
sister, a pastor, a father, a mother, a neighbor, or
whoever has offended them, whoever has disappointed
them, whoever has molested them, whoever has said
unkind words about them.

In thinking about Esau as a *"profane person,"* God
said to us: *"Follow peace!"* What a powerful command!
How are we to do that? The secret is forgiving others
so that we can be forgiven. It isn't always the big
things in life that determine what our future will be
like. Many of these *"little foxes"* are able to *"spoil the
vines"* (Song of Solomon 2:15).

Don't lose your inheritance. Don't despise your blessing. Forgive anyone. Forgive everyone. Forgive today.

Chapter 13

Joseph and Forgiveness

And when Joseph's brethren saw that their father was dead, they said, Joseph will peradventure hate us, and will certainly requite us all the evil which we did unto him. And they sent a messenger unto Joseph, saying, Thy father did command before he died, saying, So shall ye say unto Joseph, Forgive, I pray thee now, the trespass of thy brethren, and their sin; for they did unto thee evil: and now, we pray thee, forgive the trespass of the servants of the God of thy father. And Joseph wept when they spake unto him. (Genesis 50:15-17)

Joseph had a lot to forgive. He had eleven brothers, and at least ten of them had wronged him. They hated him because he said that God showed him things. They were jealous because he was a man of dreams and visions. They resented the fact that his father favored him above the others. Their hatred and jealousy and resentment finally came to a head one day, when they conspired to throw Joseph into a deep pit. They were going to kill him, but when one of them got the idea to sell him as a slave to a passing caravan, they did that instead.

But the wrongs done to Joseph by his brothers did not hinder his progress. He prospered as a slave in Egypt and was given charge of his master's house.

Again, after years of faithful service in the house of Potiphar, things did not seem to go Joseph's way. When he insisted on doing the right thing by his owner and refused the personal attentions of the man's wife, Joseph was accused of wrong doing and thrown into prison. But even the prisons of Egypt could not dampen Joseph's spirits. While he was in the Egyptian prison he was not passing his time with thoughts of revenge. He was not eaten up with resentment. He was not plotting how he would get back at all those who had wronged him. He was walking and talking with God about his future.

The pit could not hold Joseph, and the prison could not hold him either. After a time, God brought him out of prison and set him over Pharaoh's affairs. He became second in command in Egypt. Prison had not left him a broken and bitter man. He was ready for the future God had prepared for him.

When famine destroyed the plenty of the land where Joseph's father and brothers lived, the brothers were forced to travel to Egypt to find provisions for their large clan. In Egypt, they were forced to present themselves before Joseph.

If Joseph had wanted to take revenge, this was the perfect opportunity. He had his brothers right where he wanted them. They were at his mercy. But Joseph had no thoughts of revenge. He loved his brothers, whatever they had done to him. When he saw his brothers, he wept (Genesis 43:30, 45:1-2).

The brothers did not, at first, recognize Joseph. He had, after all, grown up. When they realized that it was indeed the brother they had sold into slavery, they were paralyzed with fear for their lives. But Joseph said to them:

> *Now therefore be not grieved, nor angry with yourselves, that ye sold me hither: for God did send me before you to preserve life. For these two years hath the famine been in the land: and yet there are five years, in the which there shall neither be earing nor harvest. And God sent me before you to preserve you a posterity in the earth, and to save your lives by a great deliverance. So now it was not you that sent me hither, but God: and he hath made me a father to Pharaoh, and lord of all his house, and a ruler throughout all the land of Egypt.* (Genesis 45:5-8)

All was forgiven. All was forgotten. That is true forgiveness. In time, Jacob and all his other sons and their families moved to Egypt to be near Joseph. Special land was set aside for them by the Pharaoh in honor of his faithful servant, Joseph.

Joseph's brothers, however, could hardly believe that his attitude was genuine. They knew human nature and were sure that he was just waiting for the day that he could get even. They imagined that Joseph had swallowed his pride for his father's sake. He loved his father deeply. When their father died, therefore, they assumed that the moment for revenge had come. They said, *"Joseph will certainly requite us all the evil which we did unto him."*

They were afraid to face Joseph. They sent a messenger to remind him of the words of his father, when he urged him to forgive all the wrong his brothers had done him. Jacob had done well. He was a wise father.

But these brothers didn't know Joseph very well. Their early years had been filled with the constant jealousy and jockeying for position and advantage of their mothers, Leah and Rachel. And they considered that spirit of bickering and animosity to be normal. But Joseph was different. He had learned long ago that this kind of activity bore no fruit worth gathering. Again he wept. Then, he said to his brothers:

But as for you, ye thought evil against me; but God meant it unto good, to bring to pass, as it is this day, to save much people alive. (Genesis 50:20)

And that settled the matter. There was no revenge to be had, no axe to be ground, no point to be made. Joseph had forgiven them. God had a purpose for everything that had happened. It was all for good. That was enough.

If Joseph had held something against his brothers when he went into exile and bondage, the history of Israel might have been very different. If Joseph had held bitterness in his heart against Potiphar while he was imprisoned, the history of Israel might have been very different. But He didn't.

And because Joseph refused to live in bitterness and anger, God was with him, and everything he put his hand to was prospered and blessed. God was with him because he was forgiving.The brothers had presented themselves and cast themselves at Joseph's feet, saying, "We are your slaves" (Genesis 50:18—The Living Bible). I love what Joseph said in response:

Don't be afraid of me. Am I God, to judge and to punish you? (Genesis 50:19—TLB)

Joseph was willing to leave judgment and punishment to God and to love and forgive his brothers. How about you? Have you forgiven?

Chapter 14

David and Forgiveness

And the women answered one another as they played, and said, Saul hath slain his thousands, and David his ten thousands. And Saul was very wroth, and the saying displeased him; and he said, They have ascribed unto David ten thousands, and to me they have ascribed but thousands: and what can he have more but the kingdom? (I Samuel 18:7-8)

That very day a seed of distrust and jealousy was sown in the heart of Saul against the shepherd boy, David. After David had defeated the feared giant, Goliath, and had won the acclaim of the people, something difficult to explain happened to the heart of Saul. The lad had done him no wrong. To the contrary, when the "evil spirit" came upon Saul, only the playing and singing of David could bring him relief. When the entire army trembled with the thought of facing Goliath, only David had the courage to know that no "uncircumcised Philistine" could stand against the armies of the living God.

David deserved Saul's respect. He deserved Saul's gratitude. He deserved Saul's backing. Instead, he earned Saul's distrust and animosity. Thus began a long period of unusual suffering for David, years in which he would alternately be praised and pursued by Israel's king, years in which he would alternately eat at the king's table and scrounge for food wherever he could find it in his flight to avoid capture by the jealousy-crazed king.

There were several apparent reasons for Saul's jealousy. He resented the love that his daughter, Michal, lavished on David. He resented the close relationship that his son, Jonathan, had with David. And he resented the fact that David was so blessed of God.

And Saul saw and knew that the Lord was with David, and that Michal Saul's daughter loved him. (I Samuel 18:28)

Saul began a long campaign of mistreatment of David, which included taking Michal away from him, encouraging Jonathan to turn against him and even kill him, and sending troops against him in an attempt to take his life.

David had every right to turn on Saul and take revenge for the mistreatment his king had handed out. Michal was his first wife. She was given to David in marriage after the defeat of Goliath. He loved her. Why should he lose her?

Jonathan was a close friend. They were like brothers. Why should their friendship be destroyed because of a jealous father?

Why should Saul send troops after him? What wrong had he done? Was he not loyal to his king?

The amazing part of David's story is that on at least two occasions he had opportunity to take Saul's life and refused. One night he crept into Saul's camp, advanced to the king's side and cut off part of his garment. He was sure that when Saul realized that he had been so near and could have killed him he would cease from this madness of pursuing a young man who loved him and return to his senses. He was wrong. His mercy seemed to have no recognizable effect on Saul. The king's anger and resentment only grew.

In the end, Saul lost everything and David gained everything. How else could it end? In the end, both Saul and Jonathan lost their lives in battle, and David reigned as king over Israel.

Even after Saul had died, David refused to take revenge against the king's family, as would have been normal. Instead, David looked for one of Saul's heirs whom he could bless.

> And David said, Is there yet any that is left of the house of Saul, that I may shew him kindness...? (II Samuel 9:1)

When it was discovered that Jonathan had a crippled son who was even now in hiding, he was sent for. He appeared before the new king in great fear. But David allayed his fears.

> Now when Mephibosheth, the son of Jonathan, the son of Saul, was come unto David, he fell on his face, and did reverence. And David said, Mephibosheth. And he answered, Behold thy servant! And David said unto him, Fear not: for I

*will surely shew thee kindness for Jonathan thy
father's sake, and will restore thee all the land of
Saul thy father; and thou shalt eat bread at my
table continually.* (II Samuel 9:6-7)

David appointed a family of fifteen to till the land
he restored to Mephibosheth and to plant and harvest
so that he and his family would have plenty. Is this
any way to treat the descendants of an enemy? Would
the Hatfields or the McCoys invite their enemies to
dine at their table in honor? David didn't even remind
Mephibosheth of the bad things his grandfather had
done. No wonder God blessed David so much.

David wasn't blessed because he had "a ruddy com-
plexion." He wasn't blessed because he was athletic or
had musical ability. He wasn't blessed because he understood the concepts of pastoring better than the
men of other professions. He was blessed because he
was "a man after God's own heart." It is as simple as
that. He knew how to forgive. Instead of dwelling on
the wrongs done to him, David kept his mind on the
greatness of God.

David was blessed of God because he kept well the
doors to his heart. As long as he was forgiving, Saul
could not harm him. What did he have to fear? He
didn't need to take things into his own hands and to
seek revenge. He trusted God to take care of him. And
God never fails.

David was far from perfect, in the sense that we use
that word. If anybody ever missed it, David did. Yet
something about David appealed to God, and He continued to call him "*a man after His own heart.*" When

David had some serious repenting to do of His own, God heard him. He didn't write David off. He didn't remove the kingdom from him. He didn't remove him out of his place. When Jesus lived on the earth, He was proud to be called *"the Son of David."*

Isaiah would prophesy of that key and would call it *"the key of the house of David"* (Isaiah 22:22). John would receive divine words directed to the angel of the church of Philadelphia in which he would mention *"the key of David"* (Revelation 3:7). In both instances, we are assured that when we use this key to open a door, no man can shut it. And when we use this key to shut a door, no man can open it again.

Saul was not the only man who offended David. His own son, Absalom, conspired against him and tried to overthrow him. When Absalom was killed, David wept. He didn't hold grudges.

David was a type of the Lord Jesus Christ. He was a man after God's own heart. He walked in divine forgiveness. He quickly repented when he had sinned himself, and he quickly forgave when another offended him. We have much to learn from the shepherd boy of Bethlehem.

How about you? Have you forgiven?

Chapter 15

The Prodigal Son and Forgiveness

And He said, A certain man had two sons: And the younger of them said to his father, Father, give me the portion of goods that falleth to me. And he divided unto them his living. (Luke 15:11-12)

Most everyone knows the story of the Prodigal Son, so we can skip to the conclusion. The prodigal son repented and sought forgiveness from his father. The father was more eager to forgive than the son was to seek forgiveness.

And he arose, and came to his father. But when he was yet a great way off, his father saw him, and had compassion, and ran, and fell on his neck, and kissed him. And the son said unto him, Father, I have sinned against heaven, and in thy sight, and am no more worthy to be called thy son. But the father said to his servants, Bring forth the best robe, and put it on him; and put a

ring on his hand, and shoes on his feet: And
bring hither the fatted calf, and kill it; and let us
eat, and be merry: For this my son was dead, and
is alive again; he was lost, and is found. And
they began to be merry. (Luke 15:20-24)

The prodigal son may have expected a long speech
from his father. He certainly did not expect his father
to react as he did. He was prepared to come back as a
hired servant.

But no questions were asked. No apologies were
demanded. The father was not in need of restoration.
He had forgiven his son long ago. He had no need to
question what sins the son had committed while he
was away. He had no need to require a detailed ac-
counting of how the money was spent. He was rejoicing that his son was home. Everything else was
forgotten. And, without further discussion, he called
for restoration and celebration.

But the story does not end there. There was an
elder brother.

Now his elder son was in the field: and as he
came and drew nigh to the house, he heard
musick and dancing. And he called one of the
servants, and asked what these things meant.
And he said unto him, Thy brother is come; and
thy father hath killed the fatted calf, because he
hath received him safe and sound. And he was
angry and would not go in. (Luke 15:25-28)

Some people who had younger brothers and sisters
can perhaps understand why this young man was
angry. When baby brother or baby sister came along,

Mom and Daddy began to shower affection on that baby, and the older child had to do the dishes, or carry out the trash. From that point on, they had more responsibility in the household and less attention, and they resented it. Some people have never forgiven their mothers or their fathers or their younger siblings for the offenses they suffered in childhood or youth.

This older brother couldn't enjoy the celebration. He wasn't happy that his brother had come home. He wasn't happy that his father was rejoicing. He had never forgiven his brother for running away and leaving him with all the responsibilities. He had never forgiven his brother for demanding his share of the inheritance early.

Many people are not enjoying life's party. Life is anything but a celebration to them. Many even find life so trying that they endeavor to end it all. And some succeed. Those who take their own lives, for the most part, are angry and resentful people. They simply can't find it in their hearts to forgive the wrongs done to them by family members or friends. In the end their resentment kills them.

This older son had no cause for resentment. He had not been neglected by his father. He had never lacked for anything. He had not lost his inheritance. There was plenty to go around. He had no reason to complain. Instead, he should have been happy for his brother. The father tried to get his eldest son to see this truth:

...therefore came his father out, and intreated him. And he answering said to his father, Lo,

*these many years do I serve thee, neither trans-
gressed I at any time thy commandment: and yet
thou never gavest me a kid, that I might make
merry with my friends: But as soon as this thy
son was come, which hath devoured thy living
with harlots, thou hast killed for him the fatted
calf. And he said unto him, Son, thou art ever
with me, and all that I have is thine. It was meet
that we should make merry, and be glad: for this
thy brother was dead, and is alive again; and
was lost, and is found.* (Luke 15:28-32)

When I was old enough, my parents bought me a
1940 Ford. It was a heap of junk, but it was all they
could afford at the time, and it helped me get around.
Young people today might have resented that. I was
grateful.

If something happened to you to as a child or as a
youth, you don't need to talk to psychiatrists about it.
You don't need to confront the people involved. You
don't need to confide in your pastor about it. You just
need to forgive. That's all.

Don't give the enemy anything to use against you.
Don't give him a toehold in your life. Cast that anger
and resentment from you and refuse to carry it as bag-
gage any longer. If you don't, it will make you sick and
destroy your soul.

You may think it is hard to forgive. But consider the
alternative. Nothing could be worse than being at the
mercy of the tormentor. Come on in to life's party. It is
time to rejoice in the love and favor of our Father.

Chapter 16

The Beggar Lazarus and Forgiveness

There was a certain rich man, which was clothed in purple and fine linen, and fared sumptuously every day: And there was a certain beggar named Lazarus, which was laid at his gate, full of sores, And desiring to be fed with the crumbs which fell from the rich man's table: moreover the dogs came and licked his sores. (Luke 16:19-21)

Lazarus was a poor man, a beggar. Every day he sat at the entrance to the home of a wealthy man, hoping to receive the leftovers from the table, hoping to receive something from the rich man or other members of his family or staff as they went in and out.

The rich man *"fared sumptuously."* He lived in mirth and splendor. He ate well every day. As we say in west Oklahoma and Texas, he ate "high on the hog." He had an abundance of this world's goods.

Put yourself in Lazarus' place. How would you feel?

Lazarus was considered a bother, a hindrance. No doubt people asked him why he bothered them so much, why he didn't move on down the street, why he didn't pester someone else instead, why he didn't leave them in peace.

Dogs were his companions. They came and licked his pitiful sores. They were more compassionate to him than the rich man was.

Most of us can only try to imagine what Lazarus must have felt. Most of us are so blessed that it is difficult to contemplate such a fate.

Surely Lazarus had a right to be bitter. Surely he had a right to hold a grudge against this rich man. After all, he had no social security, no Medicaid, no company retirement benefits. He didn't deserve to live like this. Didn't the rich man understand? Couldn't he spare just a little of his great bounty for a poor beggar?

But Lazarus wasn't bitter. How do we know? We know because when he died, angels came and carried him into Abraham's bosom. You don't go into the presence of God with a heart full of resentment.

This 16th chapter of Luke ends with the death of the rich man and his sudden awakening in the tormenting flames of hell. Suddenly, he needs Lazarus to help him, to send him a drop of water to cool his tongue, to send someone to warn his brothers not to live as he had. The division between chapters 16 and 17 is an artificial one. It was added later for the sake of finding text more easily. It didn't exist in the original. The first verse of chapter 17 continues the same thought.

Then said he unto the disciples, It is impossible but that offences will come: but woe unto him,

through whom they come! It were better for him
that a millstone were hanged about his neck, and
he cast into the sea, than that he should offend
one of these little ones. Take heed to yourselves: If
thy brother trespass against thee, rebuke him;
and if he repent, forgive him. (Luke 17:1-3)

Although his case was severe, Lazarus had been
forgiving. Although life had not been fair with him, he
refused to be steeped in resentment. His final destina-
tion was the eternal presence of God. How about you?
Have you forgiven?

Chapter 17

Stephen and Forgiveness

And they stoned Stephen, calling upon God, and saying, Lord Jesus, receive my spirit. And he kneeled down, and cried with a loud voice, Lord, lay not this sin to their charge. And when he had said this, he fell asleep. (Acts 7:59-60)

When seven men were chosen to take charge of some of the material affairs of the early church, Stephen was among them. When the Bible describes these seven men, most of them are only named. But of Stephen, the Bible says, he was *"a man full of faith and of the Holy Ghost"* (Acts 6:5). Later, he was described as being *"full of faith and power"* (Acts 6:8). Through his faith and power Stephen *"did great wonders and miracles among the people"* (Acts 6:8).

Many of us would like to be like Stephen. We want to be known as people of faith and power, and we want to work the works of God in our generation.

But what was Stephen like? What made him exceptional? When He was being persecuted by the people of his day, and was nearing death at their hands, the

Bible records this prayer that Stephen prayed. Bible scholars have always been amazed to see how very much this prayer of Stephen resembles the words of Jesus on the cross.

When Jesus was dying at the hands of His tormentors, He prayed: *"Father, forgive them; for they know not what they do"* (Luke 23:34). In the same way, Stephen prayed: *"Lord, lay not this sin to their charge."* It was essentially the same prayer. Is it possible that a man could have the same spirit that Christ had? Yes! It is possible! In fact, it is required. This is what being a Christian means, having the Spirit of Christ.

Stephen could pray this prayer because He had the Spirit of Christ, the Spirit of forgiveness. And that fact gave him great power.

If anyone had a reason to complain about how they were treated, it was Stephen. He hadn't done anyone any harm. He had been helping people and bringing truth to people, making them see the meaning of their long history and the love of God for them through it all.

Why should they hate him? Why should they want to hurt him? It was irrational and unjust.

Stephen, however, refused to let what other people thought and did rob him of his blessing. He prayed, *"Lord, lay not this sin to their charge."* We might have prayed: "Lord, strike them dead because they are coming against Your servant." We might have taken them to court and pressed charges against them and demanded millions of dollars in punitive damages. Perhaps this is the very reason our prayers are often hindered. Perhaps this is why some of us can't get our healing. Perhaps this is the very reason that many of us are not known as people of faith and power.

Stephen didn't give himself time to stew over what people were doing. He knew that he didn't have time to lose. He was facing God. He was face to face with eternity. He forgave immediately. He forgave so that he would have no hindrance in reaching God's presence.

How about you? Have you forgiven?

Chapter 18

Paul and Forgiveness

For out of much affliction and anguish of heart I wrote unto you with many tears; not that ye should be grieved, but that ye might know the love which I have more abundantly unto you. But if any have caused grief, he hath not grieved me, but in part: that I may not overcharge you all. Sufficient to such a man is this punishment, which was inflicted of many. So that contrariwise ye ought rather to forgive him, and comfort him, lest perhaps such a one should be swallowed up with overmuch sorrow. Wherefore I beseech you that ye would confirm your love toward him. For to this end also did I write, that I might know the proof of you, whether ye be obedient in all things. To whom ye forgive any thing, I forgive also: for if I forgave any thing, to whom I forgave it, for your sakes forgave I it in the person of Christ; Lest Satan should get an advantage of us: for we are not ignorant of his devices. II Corinthians 2:4-11)

Paul was a wonderful spiritual father to people in many of the first century cities of the Middle East,

Europe and Asia Minor. He delighted in seeing his children in victory. When he saw something that could hinder that victory, therefore, he was compelled to write them. Such was the case with this second letter to the Corinthians. Something was very wrong that hindered his rejoicing. He was concerned about the future of the Corinthian believers. Something threatened their welfare.

What Paul had to do was not pleasant for him, just as it is not pleasant for parents to discipline their children. But it had to be done. He did it with *"much affliction and anguish of heart"* and *"with many tears."* He loved these people.

The motivation behind Paul's letter was clearly not one of revenge. He didn't want his writing to grieve anyone. His purpose was not to put people down but to lift them up.

Of particular concern to him, in this passage, is a man who has erred. He does not recommend turning the back on such a brother. He does not recommend turning him out in the cold. He does not recommend isolating him. He recommends that they *"forgive him and comfort him."* He has already suffered enough.

He urges the Corinthians: *"...confirm your love toward him."* In this one act, he told them, he would have proof of the fact that they were *"obedient in all things."* If you were not aware that forgiveness was a part of our obedience to God, here it is.

One of the most beautiful aspects of Paul's teaching here is how it affects the unity of the whole Body. Everything that happens in the church does not need to produce a division among brothers. It is possible to forgive and go forward in love. It is because we feel that we must insist on being "right," on proving our point, and on making people "pay" that we cause much harm to the Body.

Forgiveness is serious business. It affects not only our own souls, but those of many others around us—for time and eternity. When Paul accepted Christ, He received the nature of Christ and the mind of Christ. He forgave because he was like Jesus.

In urging the Corinthians to forgive, Paul shows that he understood the power of forgiveness. He knew that if he was willing to forgive, satan was powerless against him. If he, at some point, would have been unwilling to do so, he understood that satan could *"get an advantage"* through the act of unforgiveness. He saw unforgiveness as satan's entryway into our lives, a portal of opportunity that must be kept shut. In effect, he is saying: "Don't let him in."

Paul didn't question the fault of the brother involved in this particular case. He just said, "Forgive him." What a person has done is not the most important issue. Forgiveness is the most important issue.

The "hurts" we harbor for so long are often for such petty things. Yet the damage satan can inflict in our own lives and the lives of our family and associates as a result of our harboring such petty hurts are broad-based. When we compare the nature of the hurt and the nature of the result, it is easy to say: "IT'S NOT WORTH IT! We are not ignorant of satan's devices."

Paul went on:

Now thanks be unto God, which always causeth us to triumph in Christ, and maketh manifest the savour of his knowledge by us in every place.
(II Corinthians 2:14)

Our triumph is in Christ, not in physically showing our strength over someone else. Our triumph is not in proving something in court. Our triumph is not in the flesh. Our triumph is in the Spirit. Our triumph is in love. Our triumph is in forgiveness.

To the Romans, Paul wrote:

Dearly beloved, avenge not yourselves, but rather give place unto wrath: for it is written, Vengeance is Mine; I will repay, saith the Lord. (Romans 12:19)

The only way we have of "revenge every act" is to be forgiving. This is our secret weapon. Therefore, we have no choice in the matter. It makes no difference what the offense is. We must forgive and, by doing so, walk in complete obedience.

Refusing to forgive will separate us from the love of God. Refusing to forgive will hinder our prayers. Refusing to forgive will endanger our souls. Those who are unwilling to forgive are dangerous to the well-being of those around them. They *"cause divisions and offences,"* and Paul warns us to *"mark them."*

Now I beseech you, brethren, mark them which cause divisions and offences contrary to the doctrine which ye have learned; and avoid them. For they that are such serve not our Lord Jesus Christ, but their own belly; and by good words and fair speeches deceive the hearts of the simple. (Romans 16:17-18)

All of this came from a man who was imprisoned, beaten, robbed, threatened, stoned and, finally, beheaded for his faith. He learned the secret of forgiving, of not harboring ill will toward any man for any reason.

How about you? Have you forgiven?

Chapter 19

The Forgiving Lord and the Unforgiving Servant

Therefore is the kingdom of heaven likened unto a certain king, which would take account of his servants. And when he had begun to reckon, one was brought unto him, which owed him ten thousand talents. But forasmuch as he had not to pay, his lord commanded him to be sold, and his wife, and children, and all that he had, and payment to be made.

The servant therefore fell down, and worshipped him, saying, Lord, have patience with me, and I will pay thee all. Then the lord of that servant was moved with compassion, and loosed him, and forgave him the debt.

But the same servant went out, and found one of his fellowservants, which owed him an hundred pence: and he laid hands on him, and took him by the throat, saying, Pay me that thou owest.

And his fellowservant fell down at his feet, and besought him, saying, Have patience with me, and I will pay thee all.

*And he would not: but went and cast him into
prison, till he should pay the debt. So when his
fellowservants saw what was done, they were
very sorry, and came and told unto their lord all
that was done.*

*Then his lord, after that he had called him, said
unto him, O thou wicked servant, I forgave thee
all that debt, because thou desiredst me: Shouldest
not thou also have had compassion on thy fellowservant, even as I had pity on thee? And his lord
was wroth, and delivered him to the tormentors,
till he should pay all that was due unto him.*

**So likewise shall My heavenly Father do
also unto you, if ye from your hearts forgive
not every one his brother their trespasses.**
(Matthew 18:23-35)

We have now come full circle. This is the passage
with which we began our teaching on forgiveness. It is
an amazing passage in several regards. First, the
story is simple to understand. There are no hidden
meanings, no unusual mysteries.

A king was going over his accounts and noticed that
one of his servants owed him 10,000 talents. The man
was called and asked why the payment had not been
made and when it could be expected. But the servant
could not answer. He was unable to pay. Because he
could not pay, he was ordered to be sold (a common
practice of that day), with his wife and children, so that
the king could recoup something of his investment.

The man, however, eloquently and movingly
pleaded for mercy. Given time, he vowed, he would pay
his debt in full. The king was moved by this plea and

granted the servant's request for clemency. But he went much further. He was so touched by the plight of his servant that he not only granted him his freedom. He pardoned him of his debt. His note was marked PAID IN FULL.

How happy that servant must have been! We can only imagine the rejoicing in his heart and his expressions of gratitude to his king. How wonderful it is to be free! How wonderful to be forgiven! We don't know how long this burden of debt had been hanging heavy upon him, how often he had dreaded the day he would face his king and possible prison for himself and his family. Now, that nightmare had ended. He was free! What rejoicing!

But the story doesn't end there. While this servant had been contemplating his possible fate at the hands of the king to whom he had owed a great debt, he had been thinking of those who owed him. How could he pay the king when others had not paid him what they owed? Never mind that they were much smaller amounts. A debt was a debt. These thoughts had dominated his mind recently. And, once he was freed, he set about to collect his debts.

Having his own debt dissolved by the king now gave him a new motivation to collect his due. He could keep what he collected. The king had freed him of his obligation.

He found a fellow servant who had borrowed a small amount from him. He imagined that the man might be reluctant to pay, so he resorted to heavy-handed tactics. He grabbed the man by the throat and threatened him if he didn't pay up immediately.

Unable to respond favorably to the threat, the man fell down before his accuser, pleading with him for time to get the money together. "You know how hard it is for one in my position," he might have said. "I will pay you everything. Just give me a little more time."

It is interesting that the reaction was identical in this case to the reaction of this man to his lord, and the response this man gave was almost word for word what he had said himself in the same situation. But the answer was different this time. The angry man "would not." He refused to hear the pleas of his fellow servant and required that the debtor be thrust into prison. He must have reasoned either that the man would never pay and would thus be taught a lesson, or that his family, seeing him in prison, would come forward with the money owed. But, in the end, he was the loser.

This act of vengeance, on the part of one who had so recently been forgiven a much greater amount, caused a great sadness to come upon some of his fellow servants. They felt obligated to tell the king what they had witnessed.

The king couldn't believe what he was hearing. He sent for the man immediately. This time he called him, *"wicked servant,"* and *"delivered him to the tormentors."*

Those final words have to be some of the most powerful in the entire Bible:

So likewise shall My heavenly Father do also unto YOU, if YE from YOUR hearts forgive not EVERY ONE his brother their trespasses. (Matthew 18:35)

What else needs to be said? This is the message of forgiveness—LOUD AND CLEAR.

What is the greatest sin? Is it adultery? Is it murder? Is it heresy? Or is it unforgiveness?

Part IV

The Personal Decision

Chapter 20

Your Choice:
Woes or Blessings

Woe unto the world because of offences! for it must needs be that offences come; but woe to that man by whom the offence cometh! (Matthew 18:7)

"*Woe*" is a word we don't use much these days. We think more of the "whoa" cowboys used to slow down their horses than the "*woe*" of the Bible. A "*woe*" is a denunciation. It is a declaration of judgment against someone. Jesus said, "*Woe to the world....*" And His woes always brought accompanying judgments.

Offending others is a serious matter that brings the judgment of God upon our lives. The dread "woes" of Revelation will soon begin to fall upon our planet. They are imminent. Those who are part of the Bride, however, will not be here to see those woes come.

In the meantime, other woes are being declared upon individual lives because of the offences being committed against our fellow man. Woe to gossipers. Woe to tale-bearers. Woe to those who are angry with their brothers without a cause. Woe to those whose sharp words cut people around them to the heart. Woe to those who bring division. Woe to those who do not heed God's call to repentance and forgiveness.

I don't know about you, but I don't want any "woes" to affect me or my family or my church. But I know that the choice is mine. It will be either woes or blessings. And I choose blessings.

When the wicked servant failed to forgive the man who owed him, after his own lord had forgiven him so much, the Scriptures says that he was delivered to the tormentors. What a terrible phrase! We can only imagine what he suffered for his failure to forgive.

I don't want to be handed over to the tormentors. I have been tormented enough in life. Why ask for more? If you are being tormented in life, this may well be the source of your problem.

If God is dealing with your heart, don't take it as a sign of His displeasure and anger with you. Realize that it is because He loves you and wants to lift you up.

And ye have forgotten the exhortation which speaketh unto you as unto children, My son, despise not thou the chastening of the Lord, nor faint when thou art rebuked of Him: For whom the Lord loveth He chasteneth, and scourgeth every son whom He receiveth. If ye endure chastening, God dealeth with you as with sons; for what son is he whom the Father chasteneth not? But if ye be without chastisement, whereof all are partakers, then are ye bastards, and not sons. (Hebrews 12:5-8)

The Lord corrects those He loves, shows them their faults and helps them to change their ways. If He doesn't tell you your faults, that would mean that He has given you up to be delivered to the tormentors.

Why do we correct our children? Isn't it because we love them and want them to be their very best and do their very best?

The word *"bastard"* is not just a naughty word. A *"bastard"* is an illegitimate child, a child born out of wedlock. Many such children have no father who claims them or cares for them. We are not *"bastard"* children. We have a loving heavenly Father. He cares enough about us to tell us when we are wrong.

It is important for us to know the difference between the chastening of the Lord and the devil's harassment. Many people don't know the difference. When God is trying to chasten them and get their thinking straightened out, they think the devil is plotting against them, and they start rebuking the devil.

God is dealing with us. Let us hear His voice.

Furthermore we have had fathers of our flesh which corrected us, and we gave them reverence: shall we not much rather be in subjection unto the Father of spirits, and live? For they verily for a few days chastened us after their own pleasure; but He for our profit, that we might be partakers of His holiness. Now no chastening for the present seemeth to be joyous, but grievous: nevertheless afterward it yieldeth the peaceable fruit of righteousness unto them which are exercised thereby. Wherefore lift up the hands which hang

*down, and the feeble knees; And make straight
paths for your feet, lest that which is lame be
turned out of the way; but let it rather be healed.*
(Hebrews 12:9-13)

God's correction brings life, while the devil's torment
brings death. God's correction is for good, while the
devil's torment is for evil. God's correction is for *"our
profit."* He wants us to be *"partakers of His holiness."*

All the blessings promised to Abraham belong to
us. All the blessings promised to Jesus belong to us.
We are heirs and joint heirs. All of God's best belongs
to His children. But when we choose not to walk in
divine correction by the Word of God, we lose our place
of blessing and open our lives to woes.

Correction, e᷑ ᷑ God's correction, doesn't seem to
be very pleasant at the moment we are receiving it. If
you have experienced it, you know exactly what I
mean. But it is short and *"afterward it yieldeth...
peaceable fruit."*

I would much rather be chastened by the Lord than
be delivered to the tormentors.

Chapter 21

Walking in Forgiveness

Be ye therefore followers of God, as dear children; And walk in love, as Christ also hath loved us, and hath given Himself for us an offering and a sacrifice to God for a sweetsmelling savour. (Ephesians 5:1-2)

When the Bible says, *"And walk in love,"* it means walk in forgiveness. Love is forgiving.

Love endures long and is patient and kind; love never is envious nor boils over with jealousy; is not boastful or vainglorious, does not display itself haughtily. It is not conceited—arrogant and inflated with pride; it is not rude (unmannerly), and does not act unbecomingly. Love [God's love in us] does not insist on its own rights or its own way, for it is not self-seeking; it is not touchy or fretful or resentful; it takes no account of the evil done to it—pays no attention to a suffered wrong. It does not rejoice at injustice and unrighteousness, but rejoices when right and truth prevail. Love bears up under anything and everything

*that comes, is ever ready to believe the best of
every person, its hopes are fadeless under all circumstances and it endures everything [without
weakening]. Love never fails.* (I Corinthians
13:4-8—The Amplified Bible)

Do you long for spiritual maturity? Then learn to
walk in forgiveness. Do you want to walk in the Spirit?
Then learn to walk in forgiveness. Jesus, your Lord,
walked in total forgiveness. Do you want to be more
like Him? Then, learn to walk in forgiveness.

When we walk in true love and peace, God will
bring other people to our feet to learn the true Gospel.
In general, people are tired of religion, per se. They
want something that will produce life, something that
will bear fruit. This world needs love, joy, peace, good-
ness, meekness, kindness, and temperance. People are
tired of the commercial message that doesn't bear last-
ing results. Will you be the person God uses to show
real love to the world?

You can't live on the fence. You can't afford to be
lukewarm about the things of God. Either get in or get
out. This is decision time.

When you walk in perfect love, you forgive in the
same moment that you are offended. You don't allow
hurts and resentments to build up in your spirit.
When you walk in perfect love, you forgive again and
again, seventy times seven in the same day—if necessary. Is it possible to love someone and not forgive
them? I don't think so.

Could this be the reason we are not seeing the
power of God manifested as it was on the Day of Pentecost? Are our "hurts" and "disappointments" robbing
us of our blessings?

Paul said to the Galatians:

If we live in the Spirit, let us also walk in the Spirit. (Galatians 5:25)

As we have seen, he went on to admonish us to avoid things that offend each other and to work toward the restoration of those who are taken in sin. This is the difference between walking in the flesh and walking in the Spirit. When you are walking in the Spirit, we not only are reconciled to God, but we work to bring others into reconciliation, as well.

Those who walk in the Spirit are not easily offended and are quick to forgive those who have wronged them in any way.

Walking *"after the Spirit"* has many advantages:

There is therefore now no condemnation to them which are in Christ Jesus, who walk not after the flesh, but after the Spirit. (Romans 8:1)

What a wonderful bonus! No condemnation! This is the life I want. How about you?

Chapter 22

Just Do It

How can we get into this life of forgiveness? How can we start forgiving? As the popular commercial of our time says, "Just do it."

If someone sticks a gun in your ribs and says, "Stick 'em up," what should you do? You should not resist. If they want to rob you, let them rob you. The loss of a life is not worth a few dollars or a watch or some other "thing."

This is the attitude we must take with the Lord. "Lord, I surrender all. I will give You whatever You ask of me. Nothing is worth losing my soul. Everything I have is Yours." When we take that attitude we can't lose. God is not a robber. He is the giver of life. The surrender He is requiring of you can only result in your blessing. He wants all the very best for you.

See Him today as He stretches forth His arms of welcome to you, beckoning to you to come.

When Stephen saw Jesus, He was not standing with His arms crossed in anger. He was eager to receive His servant. He is not looking down on us in arrogance. He has His arms outstretched, and He is saying, "*Come unto Me.*" He is calling a weary world unto Himself, to know His love and forgiveness.

His arms are wide open to you, teenagers. He's telling you:

Come unto Me. Don't let the world influence you. Don't let Satan have his way in your life. He wants to destroy you—morally, mentally, financially, physically and spiritually. He is after your generation as none before you. He senses that his time is short and that you are the last generation.

You can't fool Me. I "weigh the spirits" (Proverbs 16:2). *I know what is in the heart of every man and woman, boy and girl. You may be able to fool your parents. You may be able to fool your pastor. But you can't fool Me. I know you only too well. Drop all pretension and come to Me now.*

The Lord is reaching out to you, parents. He is saying:

Parents, you can't fool Me. I see your heart. I know your thoughts. I know those who are walking in forgiveness, and I know those who's hearts are filled with bitterness. I know those who are genuine and those who are not. Drop all pretense and come to Me now. Let My love cleanse you from all hurt and disappointment, from all anger and bitterness. Come!

Perhaps you have thought about it as you read this book and still can't think of anybody that you are angry with. I wonder if you are being honest with yourself and with God. Maybe you thought you handled a certain situation well and let the abuse roll off you "like water off a duck's back." But did you really?

Or did you make a mark in the back of your mind to be taken into account at a future date? Did you allow a tiny seed to be planted which might flourish if properly watered and produce fruit at some future date?

Are you perfect? If you think you are, you are mistaken. There was only one perfect One and they crucified Him. Admit that you are human. Admit that you have failed. Admit that you have held bad feelings against someone, probably against many people.

You can't afford to carry it any longer. Unforgiveness will hinder your prayers. Unforgiveness will hinder your faith. Unforgiveness will hinder your marriage. Unforgiveness will hinder your job. Unforgiveness will hinder your ministry. Get rid of it now. Don't give the enemy the chance he is seeking to destroy you.

Why do the Scriptures say that Jesus: *"ever liveth to make intercession"* for you (Hebrews 7:25)? Because He knew that you would need it. If you are offended 490 times a day, you need His help in forgiving 490 times a day. It is not human nature to forgive. But it is Christian nature to forgive. Let Christ work in you to this end.

Some of you who are reading these pages have grudges in your heart because someone has beat you out of some money. Sometimes fellow Christians are bad about paying their brothers. They somehow expect that they will understand. They are wrong for thinking that. But it doesn't matter. Forgive them. Don't lose your soul over a few dollars or even over a lot of dollars.

Some of you have been lax in paying people that you owed. When they tried to collect, you got mad at them. Instead of recognizing your own failure and doing the right thing, you harbor animosity toward others because they didn't just forgive you the debt.

You need to get that out of your spirit before it destroys you. You need to repent and realize that you are the one in the wrong in this situation. People have every right to collect their just dues. Get your heart right with God while you can.

You may think, "I don't have unforgiveness. I've forgiven everybody, except..." That "except" is the one we want to deal with here and now. If there is someone, anyone, that you haven't forgiven, this book was written just for you. God wants to bless you, and He can't do it in the measure He desires unless and until your heart is free of resentment toward others.

If you want to walk in the fullness of God's blessing, then you simply cannot hold any grudges in your heart against ANYONE. The glory of God is about to flood the whole earth, as God has promised would happen in the last days. We need to get ready for that outpouring. If we are not prepared, God will be forced to take some drastic action.

When He begins to pour out His Spirit upon the earth for the final time, people will die in the pews of our churches as they did in the time of the disciples. We will see a repeat of Ananias and Sapphira because the glory of God brings life, and it brings death. When the fire of God is moving, if sin is present, it must be burned up.

Don't be an Ananias or a Sapphira. Take careful inventory of your heart today. Don't leave anything unexamined. Be thorough. Make a complete pre-flight check. Are you ready to fly away with the Lord? Is your heart clean and clear? Are your thoughts clean and clear?

Time is wasting. The dread seals of Revelation are being opened. That book, which was sealed for the time of the end, is now being revealed. Time is running out. Don't put this off any longer. Deal with it now.

In order to be restored to his father's house, the prodigal son had to recognize the folly of the way he was living, and he had to repent and turn toward home. When he met his father, he had some confessing to do. "Father, he said, I have sinned." Once he had done that, everything else was easy. His father did not require penance or restitution. He warmly received his repentant son.

Jesus bid Peter to come to Him on the water. When Peter tried it, he began to sink. Jesus stretched out His arms to his servant and pulled him up from the deep water. His arms are extended to you today. Reach out to Him now.

There may be someone that you simply don't want to forgive. You know you should, but you don't want to do it. Well, if you want to get to heaven you will do it. Would you jeopardize the salvation of your own soul to punish someone for their wrong? Would you jeopardize your family by opening the door to Satan by harboring unforgiveness in your heart? Don't be foolish.

We often use the failures of others as an excuse not to do the right thing ourselves. Many people refuse to regularly attend church services because someone has offended them. Many people do not tithe because of some real or imagined slight on the part of the pastor or some other church leader.

Friend, I want to tell you something: What someone else may or may not have done to you does not justify your disobedience to God. If you are not obedient to God, you are the one who will suffer. When you stand before God some day soon, you will not be judged on the basis of what others have done, but on the basis of what you yourself have done.

Some people are so easily offended these days that almost anything you do offends them. It is difficult to be a good pastor without offending them. They are offended by what you preach and by what you don't preach. They are offended by what you do and by what you don't do. They are offended when you love them enough to point out their needs and when you don't do it. It almost seems like they are looking for any excuse not to serve God. Don't you be one of those.

Maybe you have felt, like the disciples, that your faith is just not strong enough to forgive. The Lord's response, however, to the disciples' request for more faith was instant and unexpected:

And the Lord said, If ye had faith as a grain of mustard seed, ye might say unto this sycamine tree, Be thou plucked up by the root, and be thou planted in the sea; and it should obey you. (Luke 17:6)

It doesn't take a lot of faith to be forgiving. This is not impossible to you. Believe God to help you do it, and you will succeed. You don't need more faith to do it. You need to choose to do it. If you make up your mind, God will help you do it. Don't put it off any longer. Do it today.

JUST DO IT!

Chapter 23

My Prayer for You

I want to pray for you right now—wherever you may be at this moment. While I cannot forgive for you (each of us must do that for himself), I can ask God to help you understand the importance of forgiveness and to give it the priority it deserves in your Christian life. Please pray with me.

Heavenly Father,

Thank You for Your great love toward us. Thank You for Your forgiveness. It is total; it is unconditional; and it is without restriction.

We recognize our own weaknesses in this regard. You know our hearts. We have not been very loving. We have not been very forgiving. We have not shown mercy. We have reacted to wrongs much as the world reacts. We have not been very Christ-like. And we want that to change—for the good of our souls, for the health of our bodies, and for Your favor upon our own lives, the lives of our family members and the lives of our fellow brothers and sisters.

We want to be like Jesus. We ask You to give us Your Spirit. Give us Your nature. Give us Your mind. Give us Your attitude. Let us be real CHRISTians. Let us be loving. Let us be merciful. Let us be forgiving.

We believe You are hearing our prayer of repentance. We believe You are moving right now to change our future, to change us, to change all those around us. Thank You, Lord.

> In the Name of Jesus, the Forgiver
> Amen!

Friend, it is not enough for me to pray. I want you to pray with me. Pour out your need before the Lord. He is by your side this moment to hear your cry. From your heart, say:

Father,

I thank You that I have been redeemed from sin. I thank You that You forgave me for my past life. You have not held anything against me. You have not kept in reserve anything to use against me at some later date. Thank You, Lord. Thank You for Your great love.

Now, I ask You to manifest Your love in me. Give me the spirit of forgiveness. Give me the spirit of forgetting offenses. Help me not to be so easily offended. And help me to forgive when I am offended.

I want Your fullness, and I don't want anything to hinder my prayers and hinder my blessings. I need You, Lord. I am nothing without You. Let nothing stand between us. Let nothing keep us apart.

Help me to recognize areas of unforgiveness that exist in my life and that hinder my spiritual growth. Thank You for shining Your searchlight down into my soul. I release pent up feelings of bitterness and animosity right now, in Jesus' name, and I receive Your love and Your glory.

I receive Your healing virtue into my life in the areas where unforgiveness has caused me physical pain and sickness. I allow Your love to flow through my body and to heal me from the inside out. In Jesus' name.

Jesus, You are my Advocate with the Father. Thank You for taking my case. Thank You for hearing my plea. Thank You for helping me now.

I vow to You, that from this moment on, I refuse to hold unforgiveness against anybody, no matter what they do to me or say about me. I will roll this care over onto You and allow You to deal with that person. I will not carry the weight of their wrong in my heart and be separated from Your love.

In this moment, Father, I thank You that my heart is clean. I have forgiven every man and woman who has ever offended me. I am free. I am free. Thank You, Lord.

Amen!

My Friend,

I believe that God has heard our prayer and has set you free. Rejoice in His freedom, and never again allow satan to get the advantage over you because you harbor ill will in your heart because you *allow* any unforgiveness in your heart. Take the keys of forgiveness and use them daily to loose the blessings from heaven that the Lord so desires each one of us to have, entering into the power and authority the Lord intended as we prepare for His soon return.

> Be free! In Jesus Name!
> Amen!